Behind the Goal

Behind the Goal
An Ethnography of Women in Soccer
Joseph C Wilson

Special Thanks

I want to send a special thank you to all twenty-three athletes
on the 2015 United States Women's National Team, Coach Ellis and
her coaching staff, and all the fans of Team USA. To the Aussies in
my hostel room, the Kiwis who talked to me about netball, to the
Irishman who was proud of his nation's Olympian, NYC and his
grandson, Barcelona, Edinburgh, Scarborough, Toronto, San Diego,
Nanaimo, and Shark; all five hundred people I met from Portland,
Vancouver Island, California, and Florida; the dad and daughter
from Kansas City, the clerk at the hostel restaurant, the countless
moms who refuse to quit playing the sport they love, the high school
soccer team I met on the bus, and to Montpellier who was never
more proud to be a soccer player and a woman.

Prologue

"Small Talk" Katy Perry
My name is Joseph Wilson and I am a feminist anthropologist. I focus on women's sports around the world, and- while I was writing this book- I had no idea where it would lead me. After publishing the first edition of this book, I started a multi-year adventure around the globe studying gender inequality in a vastly diverse range of sports- neither an adventure I never planned for in my life, nor an adventure I ever thought would end up defining myself and my purpose in life.

When I was at college at Southern Illinois University, I was struggling to decide what exactly I wanted to do in my life and ended up with two majors and a minor that would help me get what I assumed would be my dream job. My focus was around Native American history and contemporary cultures- and I can still name almost all of the near five hundred Indigenous Nations that call the contemporary United States home. But while I was in college, another- less official- study launched me into the world of feminism.

On one rainy day, I decided to rent the university library's copies of the Lynda Carter *Wonder Woman* TV show from the 1970's as at the time I was on a fix of watching a lot of superhero movies and TV shows. After binging on the badass heroine, I met my friends for lunch and had a heated debate of epically nerdy proportions. We were discussing the feasibility of certain superheroes, adding that Superman is an alien and is less realistic than Batman who is just rich. When we got on the topic of Wonder Woman, I adamantly stood above my dissenting colleagues to defend her realism by stating there have been numerous badass women in history who showed the same amount of abilities Wonder Woman has.

To prove my friends that I was right, I launched an entire website where I spotlighted incredible women from throughout history that showed just how incredible (perhaps "wonderful") women can be. The website led me to read Wonder Woman comics regularly, learn about historic women in feminism weekly, and- as a graduation present- to get the Wonder Woman emblem tattooed across my chest.

"My Life" Chloe Jane

About the time of graduating from SIU, I began watching the Seattle Reign- Seattle's women's soccer team. The team consisted of some of the athletes I had written about in my weekly spotlight and was my introduction into the world of women's soccer. I began watching the team as a dedicated fan in the summer of 2014- the summer during which I moved away from my home region of St. Louis, MO and started my new life in Sitka, AK. Along my journey to Alaska; I stopped in Seattle with a two-day layover, which coincided with a Reign FC home game against the Chicago Red Stars- which of course meant I went to the game.

I recall the Reign's game at Memorial Stadium well. I started by purchasing some concessions (which was, by the way, the best pizza I've ever had) before heading to my seat. During the game that ensued, the two teams hammered each other with incredible athletes competing on both sides of the field. Two men sitting next to me were even more fired up than myself as they constantly yelled at the referees when calls were made in Chicago's favor. The game ended in a draw, and I knew I needed to see more live games.

After finally arriving in Sitka- and shortly after beginning to move into my new place- I found out the 2015 Women's World Cup would be played in Canada. I figured this would be the closest Alaska would ever be to a World Cup for either gender and decided to see how much it would actually cost to go to the event. I found out the final game would be hosted in Vancouver and decided to go for it. I bought my flight, a ticket to the final game, and stadium tickets to the other games played in Vancouver.

For three weeks, I ended up living in the Jericho Beach Hostel in Vancouver in the summer of 2015 watching World Cup games and meeting soccer players from around the world- each with diverse stories and experiences of the sport. I also watched my favorite athletes play right in front of me, wrote about the experience, and returned to Alaska after the end of it all. After several weeks, I published a book (this book) detailing my experiences and thought to myself, "Let's do that again."

"Love and Run" Lexie Liu

In 2017, there was a major shift in what feminism means and what it means to be a feminist- and those changes have affected the very way in which I think about my research now. When I began writing about women's sports- and to go further back, when I began writing about historic women for my weekly spotlights- I had this idea of what it meant to be a feminist and what feminism itself meant.

When I was growing up, feminism in the United States dealt with the more Modern philosophy being defined as equality meaning the same. That two houses in a suburb are equal because they are built in the exact same floor plans with the same materials and even the same amount of drywall, nails, and shingles on the roof. This concept extended into the feminism movement of the latter half of the 20th Century and would come to be known as Third Wave Feminism.

Third Wave feminism was defined by women needing to emulate men in order to be taken seriously in the workplace- the idea that a woman must wear a suit like men wear suits in an office. But this modern form of feminism was not exactly feminine. It was built on the idea that femininity was in and of itself a crutch or a handicap, and that only by being more masculine could women be equal to men. But with the turn of the millennium, this concept began to take a different approach- an approach that played toward the more anthropological education.

In anthropology, students are taught to only judge a person or group of persons by the qualifications that group uses to judge themselves. For example, an anthropologist thrust into a nudist colony should only be judgmental of one of the citizens if that citizen actually wore clothes. So when it came down to women's issues; I began finding that as the 21st Century trudged along, the concept of feminism began to celebrate not the conformity of Modernism, but diversity and dissent- that a woman's worth was not tied to how masculine she was, but instead how herself she was.

This "Fourth Wave" of feminism highlights a period of women's rights defined largely not by equality defined through mirror imagery, but through smashing that mirror and taking pride in what makes each woman, man, and anyone who might consider themselves somewhere in-between unique. While in Vancouver, I met people from across the multinational culture of soccer who embodied this latter form of feminism.

Teams from nations with their own unique styles of play had coaches with unique issues and obstacles to overcome with their athletes. Teams set diverse goals (perhaps to compete in their first World Cup, advance past the group stage, reach the semifinals, or perhaps even win the whole damn thing). Each of them shared one common core. Each team consisted of women in soccer competing to earn the view that they deserve to be equal. At the 2015 Women's World Cup, that campaign for equality began.

Chapter 1: Pregame Coverage

"Inside Out" Camila Cabello

On 26 May, the Federal Bureau of Investigation arrested fourteen FIFA officials in their hotel rooms in Switzerland over grounds of corruption. The news shocked soccer fans around the world, and one question arose. "Why does the US care about football?" In the United States, even male soccer players fill a niche market in its sports industry. American football, college basketball, and Major League Baseball are the titans of US sports.

FBI Director James Comey responded to why the United States acted saying, "If you touch our shores with your corrupt enterprise, whether that is through meetings or through using our world class financial system, you will be held accountable for that corruption."[1] FIFA touched the wrong shores. A flood of bribery accusations ensued after the arrests. More importantly, the scandal overshadowed something else that was brewing in that 2015 summer.

On 27 May, a major media day was set for the United States Women's National Team in New York City. It was also the day the FIFA arrests hit the news networks. Alex Morgan answered questions about her ankle injury. Hope Solo asked reporters to focus on questions about the games. Abby Wambach avoided talking about the FIFA news running rampant.[2] Their "televised" media day was overshadowed by the recent corruption scandal and was anything but televised. The Women's World Cup opening game was a week away.

When I heard the news, I was house-sitting for a co-worker who had traveled with his family to California for the month. In the mornings, I was leading a fencing summer camp. In the afternoon, I was taking notes on everything to do with the Women's World Cup. It was the first time I thought controversy could exist at that large of a scale. I knew the 2015 Women's World Cup would be different from all others- one week before it even started. I had not yet known why.

---

[1] Blake. 2015.
[2] Fagan. 2015.

Meanwhile, journalist Briana Scurry argued against the media's overshadowing of the Women's World Cup. Scurry wrote for *USA Today* that soccer should be about athletes- especially with an international competition less than a week away- and not about scandals. The media had been reporting on the upcoming Women's World Cup the way weathermen often talk about cool, sunny days.

Like weathermen waiting to report on deadly tornadoes or damaging hurricanes, the major news outlets seemed to be waiting anxiously for something pertaining to male athletes that they could get excited about. The news media could have been talking about Wambach's battle against herself, fighting her aged experience to have one last victorious international title- and her first World Cup win. They could have opened up about Alex Morgan's youth going into her first international games in the previous World Cup and Olympics. They never mentioned Megan Klingenberg, Morgan Brian, or Christen Press- all headed to their first World Cup.[3]

There wasn't anyone on the major news outlets talking about any of these women. I watched ESPN for the next two days obsessively listening for the name of just one soccer player headed to the World Cup. I was having flashbacks to my childhood when I would listen to the radio for hours trying to hear that one song I heard a week before that was amazing, then never played again. Like as a child, I failed to find what I was looking for. I heard story after story about the FIFA corruption scandal- nothing more. The World Cup was two days away, and I didn't hear anything about it on TV.

"Issues" Julia Michaels
A quote from my favorite soccer player of all time recently went viral on social media. Mia Hamm once said, "My coach said I ran like a girl, I said if he could run a little faster he could too."[4] My immediate reaction was to snap my fingers and do a kind of double-laugh that sounds like a wheezing walrus. *Puhaaaaahahahaha!*" Then I realized the background to the quote was more serious than the choking walrus my laughter imitated.

In 2008, the Women's Sports Foundation published an article on the gender discrimination one girl faced- and her and her family's

---

[3] Scurry. 2015.
[4] Hamm. 2015.

efforts to get her back into sports. In Junior High, a girl named Kacy was the pride of her town. She was the kicker for the school's football team and the only girl playing in the program. Her team made it all the way to state, and she was a major factor in their success. When she entered high school, she was denied access to playing the sport she loved because "she was a girl." After months of hard work, Kacy and her parents were able to change the league rules and Kacy was able to compete in her favorite sport again.[5]

More recently, Niagara Bottling- a family owned water supplier in the US- uploaded a commercial getting to the heart of gender discrimination among young athletes. They set up a friendly match between two champion teams. One was an elite boys team, and the company told them they would be playing "the ultimate guest team." The boys weren't told they were playing against girls. Their coach- who knew the details of the set-up- prepared his team to face their ultimate opponents going so far as to say the game would test which boys could make it to the "next level."

The girls knew whom they would be playing, and- on the bus ride to the game- the girls' team expressed their belief that girls and boys are equal and should be able to play with each other. One girl said, "Boys are always saying how good they are. I just wanna show them wrong." As a side note, if I ever have a daughter and she says something like this, she will be my favorite child.

In the first half, the boys went easy on them- underestimating how good the girls were. One boy expressed his frustration towards himself for this mistake. The girls slide tackled, played aggressively, and proved the boys they were wrong to think girls couldn't play. After their loss, the boys admitted their fault and admitted the girls could handle the game and played a worthy match. Near the end of the video, one girl calmly stated, "I don't think it matters if you're a boy or a girl, all that matters is your skill."[6]

During the last week before I left for Vancouver; the preliminary games of the Women's World Cup were starting, and my fencing camp was in full swing. Everyday, I would get back from practice, take a shower, and sit down to watch whatever game

---

[5] Brown. 2008.
[6] Niagra Water. 2015.

might be on. One day, I (disgustingly) decided to skip my post-practice shower and see if anything good was on TV.

I turned on the television to *Comedy Central* to find "Tosh.0"- a show usually noted for its obscene jokes and videos of men getting hit in their man parts. The host was discussing a video of a soccer goalie that made impressive cartwheels, but failed miserably to actually save any goals. Daniel Tosh used the video as a platform to discuss how much of a joke the sport of soccer is.

He took special care to explain why American football is better. It was one thing he said during the rant however that was particularly apt for my study. He actually paid tribute to the US women joking that it's no wonder why the US women always do so well in the Women's World Cup- because we're one of only a few countries where women are allowed to wear shorts in public.

The show went even further during their "web redemption segment" when they brought in Brandi Chastain- famous for her goal celebration during the 1999 Women's World Cup when the l US won the tournament its last time.[7] For a show known for its obscene jokes and "nut taps," the episode was hilarious and surprisingly feminist. The show brought up a good point. There's something to be said about why US women dominate international sports, including soccer. In 1972, Title IX of the Education Amendment Act became law. It stated:

"No person in the United States shall, on the basis of sex, be excluded from participation in, be denied the benefits of, or be subjected to discrimination under any educational program or activity receiving Federal financial assistance."

Because public schools in the United States receive federal funding, the law most often dealt with gender discrimination in scholastic sports programs, but includes school activities not associated with athletics. The result became that most schools across the United States increased the number of available after-school activities open to girls- including sports. Since 1972, female participation in high school athletics has increased by more than 900%.[8]

---

[7] Comedy Central. 2010.

During my hostel stay, I spoke to men and women from across the world interested in my study. A woman from Spain told me girls weren't allowed to play soccer in her country when she was a child. Soccer was for men. Even today- while one can find women playing- the numbers are nowhere compared to how many boys are playing. Two couchsurfers I hosted from France said in their country, there are no sports programs for girls.

They just don't exist. A soccer player from Germany stated that even in Germany- a powerhouse in the World Cup- he didn't know of any soccer programs for girls. The same went for England, Denmark, and even Canada. The latter had some, but nowhere compared to the United States. There is no doubt Title IX is the most significant factor in the success of US women's athletics.

There is still a major obstacle facing US women in sports however. At twice the rate of boys, girls by age 14 are quitting sports. Even with Title IX, girls have 1.3 million fewer opportunities to play high school sports than boys. This comes from inadequate facilities, lack of physical education, and limited opportunities in high school and college. For girls living in unsafe urban neighborhoods, girls- understandably- prefer the safety of home to traveling through rough neighborhoods to attend practice.

There's social stigma too. Discrimination against sex, gender, and sexual orientation often prevents girls from wanting to play sports. Girls who play sports in the United States still face bullying, social isolation, and the fear of being called "lesbian"- all of which are strong enough to prevent more girls from playing. The quality of facilities is also often worse than the boys.

Girls have less access to quality coaches, equipment, and uniforms. Finally, girls in the United States are assaulted with standards of womanhood based on sex appeal. Women in the United States- according to the majority of US media- are objects to look at rather than strong and independent human beings. Many girls growing up choose to fit in rather than fight the media. Peer pressure among girls is vicious- weeding out any girls who show the slightest signs of individuality, confidence, or strength.[9]

---

[8] Women's Sports Foundation. 2011.
[9] Women's Sports Foundation. 2012.

"Confident" Demi Levato

When I was in high school, I started playing what would become my favorite sport- fencing. I was in Venture Crew- a coed program headed by the Boy Scouts of America aimed toward high-school aged participants. My dad was our Crew leader. When I was fifteen, our Crew came together to decide what we wanted to do that year. There were five of us in the group at the time, and- although it was coed- all of us were boys. We chose to try fencing, and it became the activity that defined our group. My dad had a hard time getting girls to join. Eventually, by my senior year of high school, we had one girl in the group. There were four boys.

When I got to college, my university's fencing program was falling apart. I didn't want to be part of a failing club, so I sat back and watched the program dissipate over the course of a year. In my junior year, I worked with another fencer- who did pretty much the same thing I had- and formed Southern Illinois University's Fencing Club. It was a shaky start, but noting the former club's failures, I decided the best aspect to focus on was recruiting women. It was the most difficult thing I had ever had to do.

I've backpacked through Yellowstone. I built an eight-foot tall catapult with logs and rope. I won a story-telling contest where I had to speak in front of nearly three hundred people. Getting women to join a sports club was near impossible. In the second semester, we had our first woman join. The club was arranged to be instructional and casual- giving participants the power to decide how serious they wanted to take it. All of us just had fun, and- regardless of gender/sex- the six of us in the club all had an enjoyable year.

During the second year of our club- my senior year of college- I was able to get sixty people to show up to our open house. The club members demonstrated the equipment, safety rules, and basic fencing technique. There were more than twenty girls who participated that night. Only one joined, and she became president of the club the year after I graduated. After every single practice while I walked the two miles it took to get home, I thought to myself, "How do I get more women interested in fencing?

A second woman joined during the second semester. That April, the club (read "I") organized an activity where we flew in US Olympian Nicole Ross; and it was this second woman who was the only one out of all of us to score a point against the Olympian. My hope was that by showing there are powerful women in fencing in the United States, the club could inspire more women to join.

Also during my senior year, I served on the Sports Club Executive Board. The board oversaw financial and disciplinary action dealing with SIU's forty-two sports clubs and about five hundred athletes. Most programs were either coed (ie fencing and quidditch) or had men's and women's programs (ie soccer and rugby). There were two women on the board during the first semester and one during the second (one had left for an internship elsewhere.) Even at a position of power, women in college sports were still underrepresented. I should state here that the woman who stayed on the board was the president of the women's soccer club and had been patient with my constant requests for advice on my study.

After the FIFA scandal hit the headlines and the Women's World Cup was days away, I knew my "little journal" was going to have to become field notes. I decided this trip to the World Cup would become an anthropological investigation into the culture of women's soccer in the United States. My hypothesis; "If the media were less sexist towards women in soccer, then more girls will play sports."

"I'll Be There" Jess Glynne

On 7 June, the *Washington Post* published an article on Hope Solo's controversial personal life. The article had a fairly negative view towards Solo- citing predominantly testimony from Solo's half-sister with little regard toward Solo's version of events.[10] On 8 June, *Slate* published an article similar to the *Washington Post's*- focusing on an athlete's life outside of sports. It was brief, showed shallow signs of in-depth investigation, and went so far as to accuse a separate journalist who wrote about the athlete in a positive manner as sympathizing with a woman who should be in jail.

The article attacked Solo's character, insulted her for her favorite author, called her a "reality-star wannabe," and dismissed the troubled childhood the athlete had to work impossibly hard to overcome- all while ignoring fifty percent of the story. The author even went so far as to make a game out of publicly shaming a

---

[10] Boren. 2015.

woman who earned two Olympic Gold Medals and two Golden Gloves. The article mentioned none of these accomplishments.[11]

During pregame coverage of a World Cup game on 15 June, sports commentators discussed a controversial quote from Abby Wambach. Wambach mentioned- in a way and wording that really was not controversial at all- that the artificial turf FIFA was forcing the women to play on (more on the turf later) was to blame for the US not having more goals to date in the World Cup.

A former athlete for the German Women's National Team said the German players have spoken out against the turf, but didn't "complain" about it. The commentators, a mix of men and women, all agreed Wambach was using the turf as an excuse for poor performance. One male commentator went on to say he wanted to call Wambach something he couldn't say on air.[12]

In the case of Hope Solo, Allison Glock wrote for *ESPNW* a more detailed account of Hope Solo's fateful night. Glock talked not only to Solo's half-sister, but Solo herself. Glock's goal was to get a non-biased, detailed account of what had happened the night Solo allegedly assaulted her nephew. Glock found a way to investigate the story most of her male counterparts refused to do. More importantly however, the journalist talked about how Solo applied these events to her on-the-field behavior deciphering how it would affect her performance in soccer.[13]

Abby Wambach did not receive a supportive journalist's response to her controversy- though it did pale in comparison to Solo's. What both events showed however is the state of women in sports leading into an international tournament. In the United States, the media was portraying women in sports as women who deserve to be called a bitch for speaking up against gender discrimination in facility management. The media was portraying women who worked against the world to achieve success as nothing but violent aggressors who can be mocked and jeered at for public amusement. This- however unfortunate- is not where the negative portrayal of women in the media ended.

---

[11] Peters. 2015.
[12] Fox Sports. 2015.
[13] Glock. 2015.

Gwendolyn Oxenham- author of *Finding the Game*, former professional soccer player, and current sports journalist- replied to my request for guidance in my journey to detail women in soccer. She said, "women athletes always have to talk about being a woman… while male athletes get to talk about being an athlete."[14] *Vice Sports* reported on how women in soccer have been portrayed in former World Cup and Olympic games.

In 1991's Women's World Cup in China, only two US reporters even bothered to show up. In 1996- during the first Olympic games where women were allowed to play soccer- NBC would not televise a single game. They went so far as to promise airing the final game, but went back on their promise. When the media finally did take notice of women's soccer, articles focused on sex appeal rather than athletic performance.

The article cited current USWNT member Ali Krieger who said in an interview, "You know what's great? Not talking about bikinis."[15] Mothers in sports are not spared either. Yes, women balance being an athlete with being a mother; but it becomes cliché after the five billionth article. Athletes that are women are bombarded with questions about being a mom, while male athletes who are fathers are never asked about balancing fatherhood with being an athlete. To be fair, I would actually enjoy reading those.

Leading into the 2015 games, most articles featured the FIFA corruption scandal, click-bait links to "The hottest athletes at the Women's World Cup," articles about athletes over the age of thirty-five dealing with age, or half-assed posts about women with controversial personal lives that should only matter to the people involved. How are young girls supposed to react to a society that tells them even if they are the world's best athletes, it doesn't matter? How do we get more college women to join sports when they're told to be sexy instead of confident? How do we expect women to live past seventy years old when we think it's unique for a thirty-five year-old woman to play just as well as twenty year-olds? My goal was to find out.

---

[14] Wilson. 2015.
[15] Schaerlaeckens. 2015.

"Whole Wide World" Mindy Gledhill

Twenty-four teams were headed to a World Cup that in the past included only sixteen. For many of the teams headed to the tournament, it would be a first. The FIFA website provided invaluable information on each team- especially for one particular researcher who really only knew about Team USA. On the night before the first game of the 2015 Women's World Cup, I sat down to read each country's profile.

In the 2011 World Cup, Australia (aka *The Matildas*) had the youngest team in the tournament- many of which were headed to the 2015 tournament. The team had appeared in five previous World Cups excluding only the first tournament in 1991. Brazil on the other hand qualified for every Women's World Cup, and earned a third place finish in 1999 and second place in 2007. Cameroon was headed to their first Women's World Cup. It had only qualified for the Olympics in 2012 at the London games.

The World Cup hosts- Canada- were headed to their sixth Women's World Cup. Their best finish was in 2003 when they finished fourth- the first time they escaped the group stage. Canada's Erin McLeod was a favored goalkeeper headed to the tournament. Her skills rivaled my favorite player- Hope Solo. I knew if it came down to US and Canada in the final game; it would be a game between goalies. Canada- like the US team- was not reliant on a single great player. They had Christine Sinclair, a household name in international women's soccer. Sinclair would be Canada's spearhead for offense. They also boasted veterans Diana Matheson, Kaylyn Kyle, Sophie Schmidt, and Brittany Baxter.

China was also headed to their sixth Women's World Cup, making it to the knockout stage each appearance and earned a second place finish in 1999. Colombia was headed to their second Women's World Cup. In 2011, the team failed to advance into the knockout stage, finishing the lowest in their group. Costa Rica was headed to their first Women's World Cup. Costa Rica was moving into the tournament with two veteran players however.

Shirley Cruz was a "talismanic figure" in Costa Rican soccer. She led the team with Katherine Alvarado- two veterans in a team full of rookies. Ecuador was an oasis in the Latin American teams. They too were headed to their first World Cup, but it was their coach that would define the delegates. Vanessa Arauz was 26 when the World Cup began. In 2011, she was the first woman to graduate with a coaching title in Ecuador- earning the second highest in her class.

England- unfairly- was not on my radar. I actually skipped over their country profile the night I read through them assuming, "Yeah, England will probably do all right." England was headed to their fourth Women's World Cup. In each previous occasion, they advanced to the quarterfinals. France's team had only been to two previous Women's World Cups. Their best finish was in 2011 earning fourth place. The two names to know going into the tournament would be Gaetane Thiney and Louisa Necib.

Germany was one of only a few teams that had appeared in every single Women's World Cup. They also won back-to-back titles in 2003 and 2007. Germany was definitely on my radar. Like with Canada, Germany boasted an impressive Solo-rivaling goalkeeper in the form of Nadine Angerer. Their two stars Celia Sasic and Anja Mittag would become major factors in Germany's 2015 World Cup performance.

Another rookie team at the 2015 tournament was Cote d'Ivoire (aka Ivory Coast for people who refuse to speak anything other than English). Their most valuable asset would be their coach Clementine Toure who led the team to earn a third place finish at the African Women's Championship. Cote d'Ivoire contrasted with reigning champions Japan who have been to every single Women's World Cup and who won in 2011. Japan- the only Asian nation to boast either claim- had a score to settle against the United States. In 2011, Japan defeated the US in the final game of the World cup, but the US defeated Japan in the 2012 London Olympics final. The two teams were headed into a World Cup as historic rivals. Japan played a different style of soccer than most of the world.

When most teams try to stack their line-up with powerful individuals, Japan relied heavily on smart tactics and disciplined players who act as a single unit rather than individual athletes. Goals were almost always achieved with passes at the last second, and few team members could be considered to have household names. Their contrasting style to most other teams was what usually led to victory.

If it would come down to the US v Japan, the game would throw two extremes against each other.

Korea was another relative newcomer to the tournament. In their first appearance in 2003, Korea lost all three games in the group stage and could not recover to appear in the 2007 or 2011 games. 2015 would be Mexico's third appearance in the Women's World Cup. Netherlands was headed into their first of the tournament. The 18 year-old Vivianne Miedema would be the team's core. New Zealand was headed into their fourth Women's World Cup. In each of the previous three games, New Zealand never made it past the group stage. Their coach- Tony Readings- led the team into the first knockout stage for the country's women's team at the 2012 London Olympics.

Nigeria was headed to their seventh Women's World Cup- appearing in all of them. Their best performance was in 1999 when they lost to Brazil in the quarterfinals. Desire Oparanozie and Asisat Oshoala were the big names on the team- both with impressive records and solid experience. Veteran defenders Onome Ebi and Osinachi Ohale were expected to be solid marshals on defense.

Norway was also headed to their seventh Women's World Cup. Their win in 1995 solidified their position on my radar along with fellow champions United States, Germany, and Japan. The team earned second place in 1991, and fourth in 1999 and 2007. Spain in contrast, was headed to their first Women's World Cup. Their power player was Veronica Boquete, but the team as a whole functioned similar to Japan's- solid teamwork as opposed to individual strength.

Another member of the "Seven Times Club" was Sweden. Their best finish came in 2003 against Germany. They finished second after Germany scored a *golden goal*. [The *golden goal* is a term for a rule introduced and deleted from FIFA within a ten-year period. In overtime, if a team scored a goal the game ended immediately. 2002 marked the last year of the *golden goal* rule in the men's game and 2003 for the women's. The rule was added to make over-time end faster, but it became an excuse for tied teams to play defensively- making for a massively boring game.]

Switzerland was headed to their first Women's World Cup. Their major players headed to the tournament were Ramona Bachmann and Lara Dickenmann who would go on to play major factors in their team's first appearance at the World Cup. Thailand was also headed to their first Women's World Cup. The United States was headed to their seventh Women's World Cup.

They had won twice previously in 1991 and in 1999. The lowest rank they ever received was third place. I knew Team USA would make it to the final game. It may have been American entitlement, or it may have been because I knew my team. Megan Rapinoe, Sydney Leroux, Alex Morgan, Abby Wambach, and Hope Solo were all players assembled on a stacked team with Carli Lloyd, Morgan Brian, Christie Rampone, Becky Sauerbrunn, Ali Krieger, Tobin Heath, and Christine Press. While I'm at it, I better take a moment to talk about this whole team.

"Dangerous Woman" Ariana Grande

The team itself was made up of a collection of rookies and veterans. Each player had their own unique story, and this book is 50% about telling their stories- so here is the 2015 US Women's National Team. Forward Abby Wambach was one of the most seasoned veterans on the team. She held two Olympic Gold Medals and was the 2012 FIFA Player of the Year. In the 2012 Olympics, one Colombian player straight out punched Wambach in the face, but the American badass kept playing.[16] (You'll rarely see flopping in women's soccer).

Fellow forward, Amy Rodriguez had a less literal punch in the face during her career. After the birth of her first child, Rodriguez' team traded her because they didn't want to have the liability of a mother on their team. This came after being part of the US team that won the 2012 Olympic gold.[17] Christen Press- another forward- also had a downturn in her career. After a year in the professional league, Press was traded to a Florida team; and- overnight- the league dissolved and left Press out of a job (a job that already didn't pay very well). In a last-ditch effort to maintain her career, Press moved to Sweden to play. She improved her game and made the roster for the 2012 Olympic team as an alternate.[18]

Alex Morgan and Sydney Leroux were two Olympians affected by the 2011 league collapse. The two leading forwards

---

[16] Biography.com. 2015.
[17] US Soccer. 2015.
[18] US Soccer. 2015.

joined with fellow Olympians Solo, Cox, and Rapinoe at the Seattle Sounders Women to maintain their place in soccer. Morgan was the youngest member of the 2012 Olympic team and proved herself on the field.[19] Leroux- a duel citizen of the US and Canada- proudly played for the US team and claimed her mother was the reason she continued to play the sport.[20]

Midfielder Shannon Boxx faced a different kind of conflict. Boxx had a disease called Lupus that caused her immune system to attack itself. She kept it a secret for a while- telling only her closest friend and captain Christie Rampone. When she finally told the rest of the team, they supported her in any way they could.[21] Midfielder Morgan Brian was one of the youngest members of the 2015 team. She was short enough to earn the nickname, "Plankton" but it was an unfair judgment of her performance on the field. She helped win the 2012 U-20 Women's World Cup with her aggressiveness.[22]

The free-spirited Tobin Heath took her personality onto the field every time she played. She embodied the importance of friendliness and sportsmanship in soccer, but was also a force to be reckoned with.[23] Lauren Holiday was voted the 2014 Women's Soccer Player of the Year and is another two-time Olympic Gold Medal recipient.[24] Carli Lloyd grew up playing soccer in a low income New Jersey neighborhood. She often practiced by herself- setting high expectations for herself.[25]

Heather O'Reilly also grew up in New Jersey, and growing up with only brothers made her tough. They often sent her to beat other boys at basketball. O'Reilly became famous among her teammates for her "game-face;" an intimidating face of ferocity contrasting her everyday passivism.[26] Megan Rapinoe played soccer with her twin sister growing up. The two did everything together and pushed each other to improve at sports.[27]

---

[19] Biography.com. 2015.
[20] US Soccer. 2015.
[21] US Soccer. 2015.
[22] US Soccer. 2015.
[23] US Soccer. 2015.
[24] US Soccer. 2015.
[25] US Soccer. 2015.
[26] US Soccer. 2015.

Becky Sauerbrunn had a different childhood than Rapinoe. Her brothers used to strap 2x4's to her arms and made her guard the hockey goal as they took shots at her. They pushed her outside of sports too- helping her learn how to read younger than most kids.[28] Christie Rampone had the most experience out of the whole team heading into the 2015 World Cup. She'd been on the national team for eighteen years and was the only American World Cup athlete to have been a part of a winning team.[29] Kelly O'Hara played every sport she could while growing up. She eventually stuck to soccer and became a champion youth and adult player. Her Stanford soccer career launched her into success out of college.[30]

In 2006, Ali Krieger broke one of her legs. Few athletes can recover from that kind of injury. For Krieger, it came two days before an NCAA tournament. She thought her soccer life was over. Her condition worsened further, and her actual life was in danger. She was suffering from blood clots throughout her body, and- had she waited another day to visit the hospital- Krieger would have been dead. She was only twenty-one years old. The athlete survived her surgery, and- with her brother (a recovering addict)- the two became closer than ever to become each other's inspiration to keep pushing through life.[31]

Meghan Klingenberg's working-class parents made it a point to come to as many of their daughter's sporting events as they could. When other girls were learning to dance and play piano, Klingenberg was learning Taekwondo. She brought the discipline and aggression to the field.[32] Defender Julie Johnston grew up playing soccer with her sister. She set an impressive goal for herself at a young age- to become a professional soccer player. In 2015, she was headed to the World Cup.[33]

Whitney Engen grew up in what she called a "fun house." She, her brother, and her parents were always playing games with

---

[27] US Soccer. 2015.
[28] US Soccer. 2015.
[29] US Soccer. 2015.
[30] US Soccer. 2015.
[31] US Soccer. 2015.
[32] US Soccer. 2015.
[33] US Soccer. 2015.

each other. The family play helped Engen develop a passion for soccer.[34] Lori Chalupney came from my hometown- St. Louis, Missouri. (She actually graduated from the same high school my mom went to.) At the time of the try-outs for the World Cup roster, Chalupney was a college coach rather than a player. She proved to her team she still had what it took to be a world-class athlete.[35]

Goalkeeper Ashlyn Harris grew up in a low-income family. She spent her childhood surfing, skateboarding, and playing sports with boys. She said she had to be aggressive for the boys to take her seriously. She proved how tough she was one day when she grabbed a red-tide infested starfish and slapped it across the face of one of her bullies. Her mother never disciplined her for standing up against sexist boys. Harris overcame addiction within her family and became a strong advocate for the "To Write Love on Her Arms" movement- a non-profit that helps suicidal teenagers.[36]

Alyssa Naeher and her sister grew up playing soccer, but on opposite ends of the field. They pushed each other to become better and became each other's biggest fans.[37] Hope Solo- US Goalkeeper- was not without her controversy. (Now I'm doing it too…) Solo was not defined by it though. Going into the tournament, she was a two-time Olympic Gold Medal recipient. At the 2011 Women's World Cup, she earned the Golden Glove Award. By 2015, she was considered the best goalkeeper in the world. Also, in both high school and college, Solo was an All-American athlete.[38]

The core of the team- which would prove vital during the tournament- would be Head Coach Jill Ellis. The US relied on teamwork deriving from direction via the coaching staff. On the field however, the game play would come down to players not just knowing when to follow directions, but when to go against their basic instincts. Jill Ellis could be seen during most matches sitting back on the bench; watching silently as her team played in front of her. The United States Women's National Team was going to be like no other team at the tournament.

---

[34] US Soccer. 2015.
[35] US Soccer. 2015.
[36] US Soccer. 2015.
[37] US Soccer. 2015.
[38] Biography.com. 2015.

"Lush Life" Zara Larsson

The opening game of the 2015 FIFA Women's World Cup took place on 6 June. The day before- before I read through the country profiles, researched the top athletes, and bought enough nachos and soda to satisfy two games- I bought three notebooks. Each was small enough to fit inside of the breast pocket of my "business" shirts. I use the term "business" lightly. I had three shirts that were button-up with long sleeves and collars.

I usually wore them to work- a school where I was zip-lining, climbing mountains, and cooking foreign foods. I was usually the most overdressed person on staff. In Vancouver, the shirts would be half-buttoned, never tucked in, and sleeves always rolled up. They were by no means "business" shirts. I bought the three notebooks because I would need to be able to write things down at any minute. Interviews in New Orleans during my fishing study were often impromptu conversations that I had to remember word-for-word two hours later when I reached my computer. This time, I was going to be ready.

During the pregame coverage of the opening game, I stood in the kitchen of the house I was house-sitting eating nachos in one hand and writing in my first notebook with the other. The array of former soccer players discussed the effects of playing on artificial turf. [This was the first time either women or men had to play on turf. This was because the stadiums in Canada were used for Canadian Football, which is played on artificial grass.] The five former players discussed how playing on turf is physically rougher, and tends to heat rapidly. They also discussed the FIFA corruption stories, which were rapidly growing in number and complexity.

Canada started the game early against China. Less than three minutes into the game, the Chinese goalkeeper had to make two quick saves. The Chinese retaliated with a goal kick in the fourth minute, but McLeod saved. The Canadian team pushed its pressure onto the Chinese defense, but China held strong- their goalie saving again at the seventh and eight minutes. The conflict raged on- switching sides after each failed attempt at the goal for the entire first half. At around the thirty-fifth minute, China's defense saved about a dozen Canadian attempts for a goal.

At half time, the score was still zero to zero. China maintained a strong defense, and Canada lacked the organized offense necessary for defeating it. In the second half, Canada went into a full-scale offensive. The Chinese team made saves at the seventy-third minute, the eighty-first minute, and the eighty-eighth minute. After a penalty in stoppage time, Canada received a penalty kick and Sinclair took the shot. The final score was 1-0. Canada won the opening game of the first World Cup they hosted.

I read later that day that the Netherlands defeated New Zealand 1-0. I read this rather than watched it because I was hosting a couchsurfer from France. She was backpacking across North America- having arrived from British Columbia via the ferry. (Ferries run from Seattle all the way through Southeast Alaska with stops in nearly every town imaginable.) This particular couchsurfer was traveling to Southeast for a break before returning to BC to work at a music festival.

I discussed my trip with Rennes (In this book, I will refer to people by the town/state/or province they come from to preserve autonomy and to not embarrass myself for forgetting their real names. Sorry/You're Welcome.) as we hiked up to a mountain lake in Sitka. She told me stories about what it was like to travel in Southern Asia when she was my age.

She told a story about traveling to a remote town in India. She didn't want to get stuck in a tourist trap and asked for a guide to take her to the "real" India where she spent time in a small rural town. Many of the men nearby thought she was sleeping with the village men. Evidently women in India are not highly denoted for their world traveling. She told me stories of the best foods she's had throughout her travels and about the history of the Roman Empire's expansion into Brittany. (I'm a sucker for ancient history.) During the first week of the World Cup, I was in the final week of my first fencing summer camp.

During the fencing camp, I had two participants- both students headed to high school in the fall. One was a boy who was confident in his abilities even though he had never competed in any sport before and had no experience in fencing. The other was a girl who had competed in swimming, played tennis recreationally, and seemed to have low confidence in her athletic abilities. This was not unusual. All the way back to college during my fencing programs, women always seemed to have less confidence in themselves than men.

My hardest task in teaching fencing to boys was teaching the skills. Boys (generally speaking) had the hardest time with adjusting to the footwork and parries. Girls (also, generally speaking) learned the basics of the sport fast and were actually always the fastest at becoming good enough to beat me in bouts. My hardest task with girls was building confidence. There's something in the psychology of US culture where girls and women doubt themselves more often than boys and men.

The first US game took place on the third day of the tournament. I was not going to miss it. The usual five sportscasters were talking about the US team and how prepared it was for the upcoming game. They talked about Coach Ellis and about the US past performances including the two send-of games. Commercials aired videos of US players talking about their pride of representing the US in the World Cup. In the first half of the game, Megan Rapinoe scored the first goal at the eleventh minute. Australia took the offensive testing the world's best goalkeeper. Solo saved at the twelfth and nineteenth minutes. De Vanna of the Matildas scored at the twenty-fourth.

Lisa De Vanna was born in Perth, Australia. She developed a love for soccer from a young age and claimed she used to sleep with her ball. De Vanna left Australia to play in the professional leagues in the US, but was one of the many athletes out of a job when the league dissolved in 2011. She played in various countries including Germany, the US, and Australia; but stayed in her home country after earning a spot in their World Cup team. The 2015 World Cup would be her third appearance at the tournament.[39]

Sydney Leroux switched on her war face as Team USA intensified. At the thirty-fourth minute, Wambach missed a penalty kick against the Australian goalkeeper- who went on to make two more saves at the thirty-ninth and forty-first minutes. The Australians rallied back to take the offensive, but at the forty-fourth minute Solo saved a penalty kick. During halftime- as I wore my purple Seattle Reign Hope Solo jersey- I began to think about what

---

[39] De Vanna. 2015.

would happen if Hope Solo didn't perform her absolute best at this tournament.

Americans are vicious- like the sharks in *Finding Nemo* who are kind and happy when everything is fine; but once they smell a single drop of weakness, they relentlessly attack a person's character. None of the news outlets were saying it, but I could feel every one of them just waiting for Hope Solo to make one mistake that they could use to destroy her career. That's how the media works in the United States.

In the second half, the US defense saved at the fiftieth minute. Ten minutes later, Christen Press scored against the Matildas. Less than ten minutes later, Solo saved another goal. The Australian goalkeeper saved at the seventy-third minute. Tobin Heath arose to unite the scattered US offense, and- at the seventy-seventh minute- Megan Rapinoe scored her second goal of the match.

Alex Morgan came into the game- Coach Ellis holding her back. It may have been because Morgan had a major injury heading into the tournament, or it may have been to prove to the world the US could win without the player considered to be the best forward on the team. Team USA saved against the Matildas two more times before the end of the game. The US won in a final score of 3-1. It would be one of only two games where any team scored against the US.

The following day, Japan defeated Switzerland 1-0 and Cameroon defeated Ecuador 6-0. By the fourth day of the tournament, I was starting to get an idea of which teams would make it out of the group stage. On 9 June, Spain and Costa Rica tied 1-1 and Colombia tied Mexico with the same score. On the same day, Tim Howard- goalkeeper for the US men's team- posted on facebook support for the women's team and portrayed Hope Solo as the accomplished athlete she was rather than focusing on anything else about her life. I saw this post after returning from fencing camp, muddy and wet from the rain.

During the three-hour camp, participants from each of the different activities had a snack halfway through followed by a short recess. For the last week and a half, I was playing soccer with kids aged six to twelve in the muddy field nearby. Most of the time, I just played. Occasionally I would stop to show kids how to dribble, pass, and get a good header into the goal.

On that Tuesday before my departure for Vancouver, it was raining all morning until ten minutes before recess. I made the call for the counselors to take the kids outside. I played soccer with four kids on the muddiest field I've ever played on. When I got back for the second half of fencing practice, my participants (who did not play soccer with me that day) had a fencing instructor that looked like hell.

I came home (in this instance, the place I was house-sitting at), took a shower, and invited a friend of mine over to watch the Brazil game. With six days left of being in Sitka, I was ready to leave. Brazil won the match I was barely watching 2-0 with goals from Formiga and Marta. (Brazil likes their single name footballers.) The next day, *ESPNW* posted an online article about Marta, the Brazilian soccer star.

Marta grew up in a working-class family in Brazil and had played for the country in three World Cups- four including the 2015 games. The author discussed the pay differences between male and female players in Brazil, and addressed another major critical factor to my study. Male soccer players are referred to as "soccer players" while female soccer players are referred to as "female soccer players." The media often feels it necessary to specify when an athlete is a woman, but not when they are a man- as in, men who play soccer are athletes first, but women who play soccer are women first.[40] Former soccer player, Gwendolyn Oxenham, would later back this concept.

After reading an impressive article on the gender gap between male and female soccer players in Brazil, I looked into Oxenham's background- knowing this writer had to have experience in the sport. Oxenham was a professional athlete affected by the 2007 collapse of the league. After returning to school, Oxenham and three colleagues set out to find pick-up games of soccer across the world. The documentary *Pelada* and the book *Finding the Game* detailed their journey.

I ordered the book, opting for overnight shipping so I could get it before I left for my trip- and emailed Oxenham asking for any

---

[40] Ford. 2015.

advice for what to look for. She emailed me back two days before I left saying that for her, she hated that men who played soccer got to talk about playing soccer. Women who play soccer always have to talk about being women. They never get to talk about playing soccer.[41]

On the last day of my fencing camp, I returned home in time to watch the Canada v New Zealand game. Before the game, I read that Thailand defeated Cote D'Ivoire 3-2 and China defeated the Netherlands 1-0. Before the Canada game began, I was already assembling a bracket of who I thought would make it out of the first half of the tournament. Four minutes into the Canada v New Zealand game, rain at the stadium halted the game; and the two teams had to wait thirty minutes to continue to play.

When the game restarted, it became a battle of goalkeepers. Canada's McLeod saved at the tenth minute. New Zealand's goalkeeper saved at the twenty-first minute, then again two minutes later. McLeod saved a penalty kick at the thirty-first minute, then another save ten minutes later. New Zealand's goalkeeper saved at the forty-third minute. Canada finally scored soon after, but it was taken away for an off-sides call.

After the half, the New Zealand goalkeeper made two saves in ten minutes. At the sixty-fifth minute, Canada's goalie saved, then again the New Zealand goalkeeper saved at the seventy-first and the seventy-fifth. Canada's goalkeeper saved at the seventy-ninth as the two teams fought over the entire length of the field. Five minutes later, New Zealand's goalie saved again. The game finally ended with a scoreless draw. Both teams had tested each others' goalkeepers, and both athletes proved their worth.

The following day, I read that Australia fought a scoreless game of their own against the Nigerian team. Switzerland on the other hand defeated Ecuador ten to one. Friday's USA game however was the game on my radar. Another friend of mine came over to watch the game. Both of us worked at the high school. Before the game started, two French couchsurfers arrived, also from Brittany.

(I guess people from that part of France love not being in that part of France.) They left to check out Sitka's downtown area before the game started- leaving two high school employees with a twelve-

---

[41] Ibid. Wilson. 2015.

pack of beer to watch sports. (For students in high school reading this, when summer starts; your teachers get *crazy*. We rarely drink during the school year, so we make up for it in summer. I refer to this as *Summer Mode*.)

The first half of the game started slow. The US had played their previous game similarly. They would start slow- maintaining offensive pressure. As their momentum built, the players became progressively more dangerous. When most teams wane at the sixty-minute mark, the US would continue to build speed and momentum. (They practice a philosophy in the US I refer to as, "It ain't over till it's over!") Sweden's defense was forced to make saves at the thirteen and eighteen minute marks, then again at the twenty-fourth minute.

Ten minutes later, Sweden's defense made an impressive four saves in a row; then saved again a minute later. The US style of play is also different from other countries. When most players at the World Cup hesitate just before taking a shot they're guaranteed to make, the US players take shots they have no chance of making. They'd shoot from their own goal without hesitation if they thought it had a one percent chance of going in. At the half, the score was still zero to zero; but Sweden had been hammered by the US offense.

During half time, a commercial featuring Arnold Swartzeneiger came on to support the US team. In the second half, Sweden counter-attacked- testing the US goalkeeper; but the American offense continued to build momentum. Sweden's defense was ready though. They successfully defended three corner kicks at the sixty-fifth, sixty-eight, and seventy-first minute marks. Sweden rallied and redirected the pressure onto the US.

Their best shot came at the seventy-sixth when Solo was grounded from making two saves. The Swedes took the shot. Solo was tied up in a mosh-pit and unable to guard the goal. Meghan Klingenberg thrust herself into the box and headed the ball just in time to send it over the goal- bouncing off the post and out of bounds. (MVP of the game, Meghan Klingenberg). The game finally ended in a tie 0-0, the only game of the tournament the US did not win.

After the game, Petersburg and I left to go get dinner and watch *Jurassic World*. While we were eating at the pizza place across the street, we talked about women in sports. Alaska had just recently opened a wrestling competition for girls only (it had previously been co-ed.) We talked about the role of gender in wrestling and about how our high school had some of the best wrestlers in the state. We also talked about other sports- men's and women's- and what it's like working at a high school. After eating, we went to go watch a piece of 90's nostalgia in a theater that had two screens (huge by Alaska standards). As we watched the film, I couldn't help but constantly think about my upcoming trip.

The next day, I drove the two French couchsurfers around Sitka. We hiked up to Heart Lake and rowed out in the boat there- seeing the reflection of snow-capped mountains on the murky mountain lake. I took them to see the Fortress of the Bears where the two of them took photos of five bald eagles perched within a hundred feet of us in the trees. We looked for the bears with a local family on a weekend hike.

The family gave us a ride back to the SUV I was borrowing from the folks I was house-sitting for. The dad told us about how fishing had changed in Sitka since he'd been a kid. (90% of conversations involving Sitka locals are about fish. That's island life for you.) I took the two Frenchmen to Whale Park where we spotted a starfish in a tide pool. We went out to Stargavin at the rising tide and showed them where a bear had been shot a month before when it charged a group of tourists.

I took them to the artesian well to get the cleanest water in Sitka. For them, it was an exploration of the town they were spending a weekend in. For me, it was one last breath of air in a town I had lived in for a year and was about to depart for a three-week trip in a foreign country. We stopped at the weekly farmers market to get fresh fruit, and- that night- I made them crepes they swore were better than a Frenchman could prepare. The next morning, the two left for Juneau; and I started to pack.

"Road Less Traveled" Lauren Alaina
While I waited for my laundry to finish, I read some articles on my queue. The first was a *Player's Tribune* article about Christie Rampone. Rampone was forty at the time of the 2015 Women's World Cup. The article discussed how Rampone was constantly bombarded with questions about her age. In the article, Rampone

said her real story was that she's "A Jersey Girl, a proud soccer mom, and a Springsteen fan."

She discussed her try-outs with Hamm and Chastain, moving from being a forward to a defender, the "Turf War" with FIFA, and the mystery of longevity. She also addressed why she never lets her team read articles during big tournaments. She said for every five great articles about athletes, there is one bad comment that can ruin all of them. Rampone talked about the American style of play and the importance of not comparing oneself to others.[42]

The next article on my queue was from *US Soccer* regarding *Darling Issue # 12*. The magazine (*Darling*) was founded to empower women to embrace who they are. The article featured images of the women of Team USA without touch-ups, make-up, or editing. Whitney Engen was specifically proud to sport her "farmer's tan"- something that one would not find in most images of women in magazines.[43]

A third article from *Vice Sports* highlighted Nadia Nadim. Nadim escaped violence in Afghanistan to eventually play for Sky Blue FC in the United States. The article spent a long time explaining her impressive biography, but more importantly it featured something from Nadim's point of view. She said she doesn't like to tell her own story, instead preferring to talk about her team. She said she doesn't like to look back and talked about her goal to become a surgeon.

She said she's not the ideal US soccer player, which she described as "unimpeachable, girly, spotless," and, "with ponytails." She discussed the soccer program in her resident country Denmark- the club she founded in the very neighborhood she grew up in after seeking refugee status after fleeing Afghanistan with her family. She also opened up about the salary gap between male and female players- saying the annual salary for a female soccer player is somewhere between six thousand and thirty-eight thousand per year in the US.[44]

Two videos were on my queue. Both were from *ESPNW* and featured two different athletes. The first was about Vero Boquette,

---

[42] Rampone. 2015.

[43] US Soccer. 2015.

[44] Schaerlaecken. 2015.

Spain's top player on the World Cup team. The video started with a quote from Spain's President in 1971.

"I'm not against women's football, but I don't like it either. I don't think it's feminine from an aesthetic point of view." – Joe Luis Perez Paya

In the video, "Vero" talks about how there were no girls' teams in Spain when she was growing up. She played with boys during practice but was banned from competing because she was a girl.

Eventually she was recruited to play on Spain's U-19 team and played in different countries' women's leagues. She returned to her country in 2012 to qualify for the EuroCup. The athlete missed a penalty kick against Scotland to tie the qualifying game- a moment for which she still blames herself. She refused to give up though, and scored in the last seconds of stoppage time for Spain to win. Had they tied the game, Scotland would have advanced, but not Spain. In Spain, the game marked the first time girls looked up to a female athlete as a role model. Spain was headed to their first Women's World Cup in 2015, held together by their champion, Vero.[45]

The second video from *ESPNW* featured US player Megan Rapinoe. Rapinoe also grew up playing on boys' teams, including in high school. Rapinoe explained how she never gave up on herself- even after being benched in her first World Cup in 2011. In the quarterfinal game against Brazil, the two teams were tied. If the score remained the same, the US would be knocked out. Rapinoe was thrust into the game. Carli Lloyd had the ball. Lloyd passed to Rapinoe. Rapinoe rocketed the ball towards the goal.

It was going wide. Out of nowhere like a great white bursting from the depths of the ocean towards a seal at the surface. Abby Wamabach's head appeared from a sea of defenders- exactly where and when she was needed. The US scored and went on to take second place in the tournament. Megan Rapinoe later spoke in the video about her coming out experience. Her family and team fully supported her, and Rapinoe explained near the end of the video how important it is to feel comfortable with one's self.[46]

---

[45] Mundo Sisters. 2015.

The second to last article I took notes on before leaving for Vancouver was actually sent to me from a friend who replied to the post with a tag. It was an NPR interview between Bill Littlefield and Gwendolyn Oxenham. (I was seeing the latter's name all over the place during my study.) The two discussed the differences between Marta and Neymar, two Brazilian soccer stars with two completely different careers. Neymar's salary was about $10 million US per year.

Marta struggled to find a team to play on. Santos FC- a Brazilian organization that had both a men's and women's team- fired the entire women's team so they could afford to pay Neymar. The entire women's program was cut to pay for one male athlete. Women in Brazil were only permitted to play soccer after 1979 because a law had prohibited women from playing from 1941-1979. Even in "modern" Brazil, the *Machismo* (a term referring to the highly masculine culture shared by most Latin American nations) culture continues to prevent women from playing.[47]

The final article I read into the early hours of the day I would leave Sitka was about Christen Press. The interviewer started by explaining how interviews with the athlete were "far from ordinary." The player who practiced Vedic Meditation had an "overtly psychological" character during interviews. It probably derived from her Psychology degree from Stanford.

The article discussed that while most forwards are fast and "forward thinking," Press is slower and more calculated. Press had been a top college player at Stanford, but did not make the 2011 World Cup roster. She moved to Sweden after the league collapse. The athlete refused to quit playing the sport she loved. When she played in the US, she played to win- imitating other forwards in a style she was uncomfortable with. When she moved to Sweden, she had nobody to prove herself to but herself.

Press played the way she was comfortable with- playing to her strengths and becoming better than she had ever been before. In the Australia game during the 2015 World Cup preliminaries, Christen Press scored a goal in a way only she could have pulled off- through careful calculation rather than speed or brute force. Press

---

[46] Mundo Sisters. 2015.

[47] Oxenham. 2015.

said she had arrived where she was in life by her own standards and nobody else's.[48]

In the early hours (For Sitka, it is early. The sunrise was only about an hour away, which at that time in the summer was about 3am.) after reading the *Vice Sports* article, I decided to see if Christen Press had a website. I found it and decided to click on the "Daily Inspirations" link. At the top was a poem by William Earnest Henley.

> *"Out of the night that covers me,*
> *Black as the Pit from pole to pole,*
> *I thank whatever gods may be*
> *For my unconquerable soul.*
> *In the Fell clutch of circumstance*
> *I have not winced nor cried aloud.*
> *Under the bludgeonings of chance*
> *My head is bloody, but unbowed.*
> *Beyond this place of wrath and tears*
> *Looms but the Horrors of the shade,*
> *And yet the menace of the years*
> *Finds, and shall find, my unafraid.*
> *It matters not how straight the gate,*
> *How charged with punishments the scroll.*
> *I am the master of my fate:*
> *I am the captain of my soul.*[49]

To say the poem spoke to me would be an understatement. Until I was nineteen, I had lived my life following what I thought other people wanted me to be. I was never comfortable with myself before I started college. Even in college, I was in a state of becoming comfortable with myself where for three and a half years; I referred to myself as "Spicy Charles."

There was a day however when something clicked. I decided in my life I would face failure. I would face success. If I failed, I wanted to fail after making my own choice. If I succeeded though, it would be at whatever I chose to be successful at. I had taken control

---

[48] Schaerlaecken. 2015.
[49] Henley. 2015.

of my fate. I had forged my own soul. I was setting out for an adventure into a world unknown- literally and figuratively- and whether I succeeded or failed, it would be on *my* terms.

Chapter 3: Half-Time

"New Rules" Dua Lipa

The United States played a game against Nigeria the day I flew into Vancouver. I missed the game. That completely fell from thought though while I was in the line to enter Canadian soil. Two people from China stood in line in front of me- a man and a woman traveling together who barely spoke English. The officer checking their information asked them brief questions like, "Why are you in Canada," and, "How long will you be here?" I was looking pretty solid as a fluent English speaking, white American male next in line. I had no idea.

Yes, the man asked me, "Why are you here?" and, "How long will you be here?" but things got personal. The guy asked what I do for a living.

"I'm an AmeriCorps Volunteer," I said proudly. "It's like the Peace Corps, but we're just in the US."

"How can you afford to be here?" The man asked judgmentally.

My smile was gone. "I guess I'm just good at saving my money," I replied with rapidly depleting confidence. Questions about my job, and my address became specific. There were questions about my state of origin. (Missouri and proud… to be living in Alaska.) They asked about my hair and beard. I think there were questions about my relationship status and favorite movie.

Another officer joined the man. Things were getting serious. Those two Chinese people didn't get two officers. I never liked feeling special, especially at airports. "The card you filled out says you have fruit in your bag?" the second officer asked.

"Yeah, I packed some plums for the ride. I've been on planes since this morning," I answered. It had been almost twelve hours since I left Sitka. "I can throw them away though." My confidence was completely gone. I was faltering; flopping; flailing.

"Alright, the trash can is right over there. Throw away the fruit and head on in," the first guard instructed. I was able to enter the great maple leaf nation, and all I had to do was throw away my plums.

"Pretty smooth," I thought. "I never broke a sweat."

I hailed a cab and rode to the hostel at Jericho Beach. (A map of Vancouver would resemble a hand giving the middle finger pointing west. The north folded pinky would be North Vancouver. The Ring finger would be downtown Vancouver, and the outstretched middle finger would consist of Kitsilano in the east, Jericho Beach in the middle, and the University of British Columbia in the west.)

The cab driver asked me where I was coming from, and we started talking about Alaska and how I ended up there. We started talking about the World Cup. He said it was the first time he had ever seen women compete in sports on TV. He was East Indian (he told me), and he loved being in a country where women were allowed to play soccer. He had a daughter in school that played. He said that wouldn't have happened in India.

When I got to the hostel, I stood in line for almost an hour to check in. While in line, a woman had come in telling one of the women behind the desk she was at the US v Nigeria game. (It was being played in the city.)

She said, "The US won."

"Sweet," I whispered with a clenched fist.

She continued, "I wanted them to lose though."

"You motherfucker," I thought to myself. (Summer mode, kids. Summer mode.) "What was the score?" I asked of my new mortal enemy.

"One to zero," she answered, noticing the American flag badge on my jacket.

I summoned up as much friendliness as I could to respond to my nemesis, "Well, it's good we won. Are you from Canada then?" I asked this because she had an accent that gave away her nationality. She didn't say a word. I knew I spoke loudly enough for her to hear. She was ignoring me. She stood there quietly for five whole minutes, never again acknowledging my existence.

"Wow," I thought. "Now I really am glad we won." I signed into my room, and set about putting my things away.

I've never been a big luggage kind of guy. In Boy Scouts, I went backpacking a lot. (A lot would be an understatement. I went backpacking, camping, and road-tripping so much as a kid that beds are physically uncomfortable to me. I would honestly rather sleep on a floor than a bed.) I became an experienced packer of things. When I went to Vancouver I took two carry on bags and zero checked bags.

I've seen enough people lose checked bags throughout my life that I just don't trust my belongings in that limbo world of airplane luggage. In my small duffle bag I had one week's worth of clothes, one blanket, and my medicine bag- containing toothbrush, deodorant, and hair comb. In my backpack I had my laptop, my drawing notebook, my three pocket notebooks, Thelonious- my stuffed orangutan, hiking boots, and two books.

The first of the two books was *Sex Lives of Cannibals* by J. Maartin Troost. The book is about a man who studied anthropology and creative writing, decided he was not about that student loan repayment life, and decided to move to a remote island in the Central Pacific with his fiancé. He thought it would be an island paradise, but it was in fact an island hell (but in comedy form!). I had already carved my way through half of it. The second book was the one that arrived two days before I left- *Finding the Game* by Gwendolyn Oxenham.

After I threw my two bags down on my bunk in the sixteen-bed dorm room, I headed down to the dining room to see what I could find. In the basement level of the two-story hostel sat a dining room, a kitchen, a TV room, and a café. When I went down to the dining room, I found maybe thirty 20-somethings cooking, eating, and talking. I sat down at a table to eat my inferior granola bar as those around me seemed to be having some kind of Victorian feast.

I'm the kind of person that's easy to forget. I don't like to introduce myself to strangers. I feel awkward in social situations. I *hate* crowds. I always feel like when two magnets with equal charges are pointed at each other. I stand next to a crowd of people; the crowd of people instinctively moves away from me. I sat down at a table in a crowded room of people who completely avoided contact with me, and I ate my Clif Bar dinner in silence. I might be the worst socio-cultural anthropologist in the world.

I left the dining room and went to bed. I was exhausted and needed to do something to get me out of that room. That night, I slept for twelve hours. This is actually fairly common for me. (Don't ask me to do something before 9am. I won't do it.) I gave myself two days of "vacation" in Vancouver; two days where I could have a brief amount of fun before I got down to work- the tedious, horrible work of watching and talking about sports all day, everyday, for three weeks. (The things I do for research…)

In the afternoon, I took the bus into town to check out a cool comic book store I had heard about. It was a small shop overfilled with bins of old comics. If I haven't made it clear yet, Wonder Woman is my favorite superhero. I spent an hour looking through the small store, and I found one action figure of the hero; an action figure I already own. I felt bad for perusing the store, so I settled on buying a Captain America toy for ten bucks. He is my *second* favorite superhero. I sat down in a Korean bakery across the street and ate my cantaloupe cake as I played with my new action figure and forgot I was twenty-four years old.

I returned to the hostel before teatime and thus found myself drinking a cup of jasmine green tea out of my Wonder Woman travel mug in the hostel dining room. I contemplated a paper flier hung up across from the front desk. It advertised a weekly pub night starting in four hours. I decided anything would be better than sitting in a room full of people ignoring my presence and elected to hop on the bus again and head downtown.

The pub night brought together residents from four different hostels throughout the city- united by a single company. Maybe twenty people showed up- all in their twenties with the exception of two nineteen year olds. We had one guide. Our first bar was *Doolin's* which would become my unofficial home in Vancouver. (As a descendent of Irish ancestors, I often use the shade of a pub as sunscreen. We're like vampires, but we drink pints of beer instead of pints of blood.) At the long table in *Doolin's* I took to talking with two Australians, a Brazilian, a Frenchman, and three Americans.

An American man who had just graduated college led the conversation. He had hemp rope bracelets covering his entire left forearm. I was wearing my red bead bracelets. We both had beards. When this kind of thing happens, there are usually two results. An Old West style duel erupts in a "There can only be one bearded man with bracelets in this town," or it becomes an epic night of two bearded men with bracelets hanging out with other awesome people after skipping out on a pub crawl. It was the latter.

We four Americans, the Frenchman, and the two Australians hit up a liquor store and headed back to the main hostel (Central) and had our own night. The Australians told stories of drinking games.

One of the American women was in Vancouver for her 19th birthday and shotgunned a beer for her coming of age ceremony. As the anthropologist I am, I video recorded the latter for future generations. The coming-of-age ceremony for residents of the state of Washington evidently involves traveling to British Columbia where the drinking age is nineteen, getting completely inebriated on said birthday, then returning home with a wicked headache we employed folks like to call, "a reason not to go to work today."

After talking for over three hours, I finally decided to get back on the bus and headed back to my hostel. I sat on the bus for thirty minutes, leaving behind the first real conversation I had in Vancouver. I scribbled in my notebook everything I could remember. I didn't write anything down during the encounter. I never did while in Canada. Someone asked me later why, and I told her that it usually makes people say things they wouldn't normally say. I prefer having a casual conversation, then writing down what I can remember. That way, I get to hear what people truly wish to talk about. When I got back to the hostel, I put away my notebook and went to sleep.

On my second of two vacation days in Vancouver I set out to explore a gem of Vancouver's *alternative* side. To the immediate west of the University of British Columbia sits a crescent beach half-surrounding the campus. This beach was called Wreck Beach, and it was what one sign referred to as "Clothing Optional." One might think this means it is a nude beach, but that would be wrong. Wreck Beach was a nude beach for men over the age of 40 who like to walk up and down the beach eyeing women who keep their clothing on to protect their lady parts from the gaze of said ogling middle-aged men.

I sat down, took my shirt off- keeping everything else on- and read *Sex Lives of Cannibals*. The beach was quiet. I like quiet. Quiet means there's no one magnifying away from me. It means I can read a book and not have to listen to five million people. Quiet means I'm alone because there are no people around, not alone because the people around are ignoring me. I sat long enough to read the third quarter of the book before the sight of a man selling what I can only describe as "hippy blankets" caught my attention.

I figured, "I got this blanket at a nude beach!" would be an excellent thing I could say on my return to Sitka.

The salesman had assembled a blanket fort out of his merchandise. Different blankets and shirts cost different amounts, but all of them were cheap. I bought the blanket for ten Canadian, left the beach, and stopped at a café on campus for a soda. I sat there in my half-buttoned shirt wearing three bracelets and two necklaces. The blanket was draped over my shoulders. *Sex Lives of Cannibals* was set before me on the table.

My hair- unkempt from a day of lying on the beach fell wavy and knotted down to my shoulders. As I noticed the people around me attempting to stare inauspiciously- and failing- I thought to myself, "I've become my Uncle Pat. I'm okay with this." (My uncle was a stagehand at Woodstock.) After finishing my soda, I walked back to the hostel, wrote notes, and took a four-hour nap.

I sat down in the TV room where the dark room was contrasted by the light of the television. From inside, two others sat talking about where they were from. The first was a man from Australia. The second was a man from California who was highly intelligent in foreign politics. He asked the Australian about his prime minister. The Australian said how he felt- aka, "the guy has no idea what he's doing and should not be prime minister."

I opened up that I'm also from the States, and the three of us talked about life in three distinct places. The Australian said he was in Vancouver for work. I said I was in Vancouver for research. The Californian said he was in Vancouver because he's a "hustler" and decided to visit the city for the "hell of it." (You have to respect an honest man.) I spoke to the Californian after the Australian left.

He was African American, and- after I told him I was from St. Louis- he asked about the recent race issues there. He asked an important question I could not answer. "Why do white people like black culture, but hate black people?" I still can't answer this question. Someone really needs to find out. (Get on it, America!) After heading to bed, I fought insomnia until three in the morning before finally falling asleep.

"Drinkee" Sofi Tukker

My two days of allotted vacation days were over and I had an appointment to make. On Friday the nineteenth, I had a meeting with an anthropology professor at the University of British Columbia. The plan was to meet up at the Museum of Anthropology on campus then talk about my study. I guess Canadians aren't known for keeping appointments. I arrived at the museum two hours early. I hate being late for things. I'm the guy that shows up to a party early. Actually, I once showed up to a party before the host showed up; that was weird. In this instance, I wanted to tour the museum. After all, I am an anthropologist (albeit, an anthropologist with only a bachelor's degree who happened to be conducting my own field study out of pocket with no university support), and I wanted to check this place out.

In Sitka, the Native People are the Tlingit. (I should note here, most people mispronounce this name and even the more accurate version I use is still a butcher of pronunciation. Tlingit, for us white folk, is pronounced *Klinket*; and that's the best way I can advise one pronounces it.) The Native People of the Vancouver area were the Haida. The Tlingit and the Haida- both Northwest Coast Peoples- for a long period were enemies- a rivalry that put Cardinals and Cubs fans to shame. The museum featured enough artifacts from the Haida to occupy half of the floor space. The other half consisted of artifacts from Asia, Africa, Oceania, and Europe. I spent most of my time eyeballing the Haida art, which very closely resembled that of the Tlingit.

The art of both involves everyday items that have been masterfully crafted from carved wood with intricate painted figures known as *formline*. These items can be as small as soup ladles and as large as meetinghouses. As I walked through the isles of the museum, my eyes caught the sight of two items that stood out from the rest. One was a hockey jersey and the other a snowboard.

After reading the signs posted below them, I found out they were artifacts from the Vancouver Winter Olympics. The hockey jersey had the maple leaf of Team Canada with Haida formline images inside. The snowboard featured Haida formline as well, with imagery granting health and luck to the athlete who used it. The two items were evidence that there's a place for sports in anthropology, and I started to feel like I was actually doing something relevant.

I sat down in the museum café and waited for the professor to arrive- for more than an hour. I checked my email every ten minutes waiting to hear from him, but there was nothing. I finally went to his office in a building across a garden from the museum. His office was closed, but I found an open door across the hall and explained the situation with the professor there. After leaving a note under the door, I left UBC and never went back.

Finding a contact can be difficult. I usually try to find professors at local universities with backgrounds that most match what I'm studying. They are usually great sources for finding out where to begin research, where to find people to interview, and what books I should read. Of course, doing it all on my own made the whole situation more self-made and inevitably led me to taking great pride in my research.

When I returned to the hostel, I stepped inside the restaurant for dinner. The café was more diner than coffee shop. There were booths and tables taking up most of the space and an "L" shaped bar that housed the register. A sign on the wall stated the restaurant was a feature of a local culinary school that trained chefs how to work in the food service. Two other signs listed the menu items for breakfast and lunch/dinner. As I sat at the bar eating my dinner, I talked to the clerk about why I was in Vancouver.

Turns out he was a big soccer fan who- like me- preferred the women's team to the men's because of their international record. (Canada's women's team was favored to reach the finals. Canada's men's team has rarely made it to a World Cup.) We also talked about women in other sports and the connection between women's rights worldwide and how it reflected in a team's performance at international competitions. The *Tosh.0* joke was suddenly a lot more accurate than predicted.

The second of the two adventures that carried me into my research is one I do not fully remember. It started out as what was supposed to be lunch with a fellow comic book fan and world traveler. It turned into a night that would make my Irish ancestors proud. To the best that I can remember, the following is an account of what happened on Saturday, 20 June.
In the morning, I went down to the hostel restaurant for breakfast. When I returned to my bunk, I finished reading *Sex Lives of Cannibals*, gathered change for the bus, then set off for the city. I met a *couchsurfer* at a skytrain station. He was an athletic Canadian wearing a thermal long-sleeve shirt with a watch that showed his economic status. (Wealthy)

After our introductions, he took me to one of his favorite restaurants in Vancouver- a place he frequented for lunch. When we sat down, an attractive woman in a black, form-fitting dress waited on us. I felt underdressed. It was a Saturday, which means I was probably wearing either a Doctor Who t-shirt or my t-shirt that resembles a pair of lederhosen. I know I was wearing shorts with socks that most likely had corgis in sunglasses on them. (I swear I'm an anthropologist.)

After ordering our food, Vancouver and I got to talk about comic books. We had a lengthy conversation about Wonder Woman and the actress who would be portraying her in the *Batman vs Superman* movie. (By the way, as a man with the Wonder Woman emblem tattooed across his chest, I feel like I can claim to be an authority on the hero. Gal Gadot is amazing as Wonder Woman.) We talked about the *Arrow* and *Flash* TV shows. We joked about the *Supergirl* previews.

Then, I asked the question, "So, do you play any sports?"

Vancouver was a Division Three soccer player. I had to think about this in baseball terms. Division one is comparable to the Major Leagues. That would be Shannon Boxx and Lauren Holiday. Division two is comparable to the minor league. Division three is high enough to warrant international games, but small enough to prevent the athlete from having to make the sport his/her career.

I was sitting with an athlete. I told him about my study, and he invited a couple of his friends to join us. While we waited for his friends, Vancouver continued and explained professionally, he's a game designer. He spoke proudly of his most recent project- designing the female athletes in the new FIFA game. The FIFA 2016 video game would feature female players for the first time. I was speaking to one of the people who helped make it happen. Vancouver's friends arrived.

They too were athletes and comic book fans. All three of them were proud of Canada's Women's National Team and what they were doing for young girls in Canada. They all agreed they wanted to see more women in Canada playing sports and cited the woman who left Canada to play for a professional hockey team in the US. (One of the three was a hockey player.) Just before we left the restaurant, in a parting shot really, I asked the waitress if she played sports.

"No," she replied. "Why, do I have an athlete's body?"

"Oh, no," I returned. "I asked because I'm researching the role of women in sports."

The four other guys tried to learn more about why the waitress didn't play any sports. She replied that she started smoking when she was a teenager and didn't want to try playing any sports. She left the table, and the five of us left the restaurant. We walked into a jazz festival- because I guess this sort of thing just happens in Vancouver- and after listening to what was either post-modern jazz or a group of musicians warming up, we left the crowd and headed towards the nearest comic book store.

Inside the densely trafficked shop, the five of us split and scoured the store for items worth purchasing. I wound up on the second floor where discounted items sat on shelves. I found a Wonder Woman book of collected comics from the forties. Ten dollars. Obviously, I bought it. The other guys noticed two corsets hanging high on the wall. One was a Supergirl outfit, the other Wonder Woman.

I was happy with *my* purchase. One of the other four guys texted his girlfriend a photo of the two outfits. We left the store and headed to get food. I suddenly thought of Odysseus and his epic tale of trying to reach home to find his family. I was thinking about trying to reach my hostel to find a positive bank account. A night out on the town, in Vancouver or Sitka, is not easy on a volunteer's salary. I was with people I could learn from though, and decided it was in my best interest to keep going. (One-eyed giants and island witches, here I come!)

We stopped into a restaurant called "The Factory" where one could buy anything on the menu for five dollars. This kind of place is the kind that foreshadows a grim evening ahead. I got wings and a tall boy, and the five of us got back onto the topic of sports. The Canadians were talking about the players on Canada's team and what they would have to do to win the World Cup.

"They'll need Sinclair," said one of them.

"And Kyle," said another.

"That's Kaylyn Kyle?" I asked.

"Yeah," he returned. "We'll need her."

We talked about which players would need to be in the starting line-up in Canada's upcoming games if the team was going to make it to the final. Only after talking about athletes for what had become up to that point nine hours did we talk about the physical attractiveness of some of the World Cup soccer players. We spoke of the subject for ten minutes, and then moved on.

"So and so is pretty hot," said one of us.

"Yeah, so is that one American player," said another.

"Oh yeah yeah," spoke a third.

Then we went back to eating and finished our food. When the bus boy (Or bus girl? Is this a legitimate term?) at The Factory came by to pick up our dishes, I asked her, "Do you play any sports?"

"Um, I used to," she returned briefly as she loaded dishes into her bucket.

"Do you still play?" I continued.

"No, I quit a long time ago," she replied.

"May I ask why?" I investigated.

She looked at me and spoke, "I grew up."

She walked away in my silent response. I started contemplating if sports- in Canada- was a perfectly acceptable world for girls, but that this social acceptance ended once a girl grew up. When I was a senior in college, I got Wonder Woman's emblem tattooed across my chest. Whenever I am in a situation where I can sense a strong, independent woman nearby; I can feel my tattoo. (I'm not lying. It's like when an amputee gets the ghost limb and can feel their missing foot or hand.) I felt my tattoo when the bus boy walked away.

Women who quit sports don't do it because they're weak. They do it because it's a choice a person has to make- man or woman- and having to choose between doing something one loves and something that earns a person a living is a choice too many adults have to make. I made that choice. I chose what I love. I was *broke*. I wasn't "Oh, I need to save my money" broke. I was "I need to have a serious discussion with my landlord this month" broke. I will never claim people who choose making a living over doing what they love made the wrong choice.

I was convinced I needed to stay with this group of knowledgeable athletes. My bank account be damned. The five of us left and met up with a sixth on our way to a bar in the old cobblestone-y part of Vancouver. It was an Irish pub. The Canadians told me an Irish band would be playing, and I hadn't heard the sound of a live Irish band in nearly two years. I had high expectations.

After sitting down, I decided the best thing for me to do would be to drink water.

I was not about to show up at the hostel completely wasted at two in the morning. Unfortunately that's exactly what happened. When the waitress brought us all our drinks, I had to ask her about the décor of the pub. It was suspiciously anti-Ulster. The band was playing songs I had never heard before. (I was raised on Irish music. If an hour of music claiming to be Irish plays and I don't recognize any of the songs, it's not Irish.)

"Can I ask you a question?" I started. "You have three shields, and a space for a fourth, but the fourth shield isn't there." The shields were three of the four shields of the kingdoms of Ireland. (Leister, Connacht, and Munster.) The missing shield was the Ulster shield. Part of Ulster is controlled by the UK and is known as Northern Ireland. I can understand the disagreements between Ireland (Republic) and Northern Ireland (region of the UK), but because the Republic of Ireland controls part of Ulster, refusing to include the Ulster shield is just silly.

She looked at the blank, naked nail then looked back at me. "Oh, I don't know. Are there supposed to be four shields?" This person did not know about the four kingdoms of Ireland. When she left, I explained my plight with the others. I determined this was the sort of "pub" that liked to prey on the unsuspecting tourists claiming to be an Irish pub, but which didn't carry such things as Harp or Smithicks. I determined this was not an Irish pub.

There is no shame then in saying that I had to be escorted out of the bar by the owner. After playing drinking games with the Canadians, I wound up in the washroom setting the new standard for "puke free since…" The owner of the bar picked me up and walked me out leaving me sitting on the curb with a bottle of water. The Canadians found me, brought me my effects, hailed me a cab, and paid my fare. (Big thanks, guys!)

I somehow managed to reach the hostel after switching cabs half-way through, made it past the front desk without making (too much) of an ass of myself, got into my bed, went to the washroom (let's just go with "to take care of things"), returned to bed, and blacked out. This was at least the story the Aussies in the room told me after I needed a refresher course on exactly how I miraculously found my bed that night. (Thank you, Aussies.)

"You Need To Calm Down" Taylor Swift

After waking from a twelve-hour sleep, I stumbled into the TV room to watch the Canada v Switzerland game. I didn't take notes on the game, mostly because the feelings in my stomach and head prevented me from thinking clearly enough to remember my notebook. I did however talk to the two people watching the game with me. The game was slow anyway. Canada won 1-0. After the game, I had finally built up enough strength to eat food and drink copious amounts of hot coffee. (Tequila bad. Coffee good.)

I spoke with the clerk again about soccer. I told him his country beat Switzerland, and it led to him talking about how much he prefers women's soccer to men's because of Canada's record in both. We also talked about golf- a sport I myself have never watched. I can appreciate the sport, but it is something comparable to paint drying when watching. After leaving the restaurant, I fetched my second book from my bed and headed down to the dining room. I read *Finding the Game* until one in the morning before finally heading to sleep after one of the worst hangovers I'd ever had.

On Monday the twenty-second, I woke at a respectable hour (11am), took a hot shower, and made my way down to the TV room for the Norway v England game. The game drew quite a crowd in the hostel TV room. Four Canadians, a German, a couple Australians, and a couple of folks from France sat in to watch. Norway was favored to win. During the game, I spoke to those in the room. The German man said he played soccer in Germany and watched the men's games; boasting of his country's win at the World Cup the year before. Without me needing to ask, the German told me his thoughts on women playing.

"They're not very good," he spoke bluntly. "And I don't mean they never will be." I asked him to explain further. "These women probably started playing five or six years ago," he responded. "Men in Germany have been playing since they were five or six."

"So girls need to start playing at that age?" I asked.

"Yeah," he returned. "And not just some. There needs to be a lot of girls playing from that age."

I continued, "A bigger pool of players you mean?"

"Yeah, you need a larger group to choose the best from," the German replied.

I voiced my own opinion, "Because there could be a natural out there. A girl who could be destined to be the best soccer player in the world; and if she doesn't start playing as a kid, that best player will never enter the sport."

"Exactly," the German agreed. He continued, "And I think it's great that women get to play a sport people associate with men, but then there's men who play in women's sports." I let him continue, interested to hear him explain further. "Like gymnastics," he spoke. "Men who are in gymnastics are stereotyped as being gay. And there's nothing wrong with being gay, but that could still keep a boy from wanting to do it."

This is a topic rarely discussed in feminism. It's one I actually wish was addressed more often. Men are the victims of sexism just as much as women. Boys grow up hearing, "Be a man!" We're called pussies when we're weak- meaning the worst insult a man can receive is being associated with being a woman. There's also stereotypes that if men care about fashion or interior decorating, or rhythmic gymnastics; that they're gay. There is nothing wrong with being a woman. There is nothing wrong with being gay. These associations however are ingrained in American society to the point that it can cause any boy or man of any age to quit doing something they love in fear of ridicule.

The French woman in the room added to the conversation. "I play soccer in France," she explained. "I also lead a soccer camp. It's for children under nine years old, and I get boys and girls. The boys always tell their dads their instructor is a girl, and I have to prove I'm good enough to teach their sons how to play."

In the United States, women have to prove themselves all the time. An athlete that's a mother has to prove she can still play after having a child. A father doesn't. A woman over the age of thirty has to prove she can still dominate at her sport. A man doesn't. The French woman was proof that even a person who teaches a sport to five year olds had to prove she could play soccer to a sexist father.

I was so caught up in the conversation that I saw only glimpses of the game. England defeated Norway 2-1. It was the next game I had woken up for. Before it began, I ran up to my room to grab my jersey. I walked back down the stairs to the TV room proudly sporting my favorite soccer player's shirt. Most of the people in the room had left. I didn't care. I was there to watch my country defeat Colombia.

One of the Colombian players the day before had accused Team USA of "belittling" them. Lady Andrade of Colombia spoke of the US team members disrespecting her team. Lady Andrade was the athlete that punched Abby Wambach in the middle of an Olympic match in 2012. Coach Ellis and athlete Alex Morgan responded to the accusations in *USA Today*.[50]

During the pregame coverage, Hope Solo's private life was addressed. Actually, I should explain that a female anchor on *Fox Sports* addressed Solo's private life to a male field reporter. The male reporter- in a completely surprising move- told the female anchor that Solo is an athlete, and that it's her role as an athlete that should be addressed. He spoke about her athletic record citing her career achievements without talking about her personal life. Another American joined me to watch the game. The football/basketball player told me during the halftime that she prefers playing sports with men.

"Women," she told me, "are more likely to foul. They get vicious."

"Really?" I asked.

"Yeah," she continued. "I guess they feel like they need to prove themselves. The guys just play to play. The girls play to prove they're good enough to play." We continued to talk about the subject, mostly repeating things we had already said in different words. The athlete told me she also thought women had less "boundaries" than men. They're willing to play dirtier because the athlete thought women don't play by the same unofficial rules than men play with.

I immediately thought of every time I play basketball. I'm terrible at shooting, so I make up for it by playing hard defense. Most people I've played with however don't. There's an unofficial rule in pick-up games of basketball where the only acceptable defense is simply trying to intercept passes. Standing closer than one foot away from an opposing player is considered cheap. I don't play very often, so it took me about two years to figure this rule out.

---

[50] Rogers. 2015.

I figured the athlete I was talking to was referring to people who don't play pick-up games often and are unaware of the unofficial rules of play, and that these people happened to be primarily women. The game ended in a 2-0 victory for the United States, and I celebrated calmly. I spent my competitive years in fencing understanding an early victory was not the one to celebrate. The US had only made it into the quarterfinals. I would celebrate only a total victory.

Chapter 4: Second Half

"Level Up" Ciara

Way far back in November, I purchased the stadium half-pass to BC Place. This meant I had tickets to half of the games at the stadium and a ticket to the final game was mine for a discount. The total cost of three games plus the final was four hundred and fifty Canadian dollars. I ended up donating my first ticket- a game in the preliminaries when I was still in Sitka teaching teenagers how to fence. The second ticket was for the Japan v Netherlands game of the round of sixteen. I did not donate that ticket.

I thrust myself on the bus into the city and found myself a seat. I found fellow game-goers on the bus- a whole family headed to watch the game. They had the same pass I had. With the family were three kids who played soccer- two boys and one girl- along with a woman in her thirties who continues to play. We talked about my study. They talked about what it's like to play the game. The woman explained what it's like playing with women half her age. Before we got off the bus, they showed me a photo that made me infinitely jealous; a group photo with Abby Wambach.

After a brief foré into a pub beside the stadium (there's that Irish sunscreen I was talking about), I walked into the stadium and found my seat. My seat was just to the left behind the north goal. Up to this point I had thought about what to name my study for sometime. New names were hitting me about three times a day, but none of them ever clicked. I took a photo of where I was so I could brag to all of my friends, and- when I lowered my phone- I thought, "Behind the Goal- hey, that's actually pretty good."

When the teams first took the field to warm up with their coaches, the two people with seats next to me found their places. I struck up a conversation with the father and daughter to find out they were from Kansas City and also had the half-pass. The daughter was in high school and was the most knowledgeable person I had ever met in the field of women's soccer. We talked about my study- a conversation that repeated nearly three or four times per day- and watched the players retreat from the field to prepare for the game.

There was a ritual to how these games would begin. When the players sat in the locker rooms to prepare for the game ahead, the crew of the stadium watered the field one last time. This was done to prevent injuries from dry plastic and overheating. Next, the ball-ushers (This term I admittedly invented. This group of female game ball bearers that look like they were in high school stood surrounding the field with soccer balls at the ready to throw in at any moment's notice.) took their positions with special soccer balls decorated uniquely for the 2015 World Cup.

Two giant flags born by a team of a dozen bearers per flag descended onto the field in front of the two teams as their starting players paraded onto the field with one young girl per player standing before them. The national anthems of both nations were played followed by the "Handshake for Peace" signifying the beginning of a fair and friendly game. Once the press photographers took their positions, athletes were introduced, referees were revealed, and the game could start.

During every Japan game- no matter the location- there was always at least one Japanese fan drumming on a parade drum. For the entirety of every game, this nameless drummer pounded away in a beat that echoed across the stadium. The "Oh!'s" of excitement provided a perfect chorus to the percussion. At the tenth minute, Ariyoshi of Japan scored the first goal. Japan had great control of the ball- almost taunting the Netherlands into attempting to get a hold of it in a game of "carrot and stick."

The Netherlands relied on its center players- center forward, center midfielder, center defender, and goalkeeper. It was their biggest mistake. To prevent Japan from getting the ball- the few times Japan lost control of it- Netherland's players kept passing the ball to their goalkeeper; and Japan adapted quickly. The Dutch goalkeeper had to play more than any other single player in that game.

During half time, stadium security took their positions. A student at UBC stood next to me. He was working at the stadium during the tournament and was a kinesiology student nearly finished with school. We struck up a conversation, and- when I mentioned my study- he smiled and looked up to the high seats. "I just wrote a paper on the self-esteem of female athletes," he spoke. "And why a lot of girls quit sports."

This was the second time I felt like my research had a place in the world. He pointed to the field where crews were watering it during the break. "They're doing that to prevent injuries. It gets hot enough that they need to water it." Then he left, heading back to his position during game-play; and it was the only time I spoke with him.

For the second half- as with every game- the two teams switched sides, and I was able to see the look on Dutch players' faces when they went for the goal. I want to say how much of an honor it was to be where I was during this game- not for the prestige of the seat, but for the opportunity it gave me. The Japanese goalkeeper had some mad skills during that game that I cannot refute, but it did not win the game. The Japanese won the game because Dutch players did something most players in the tournament did; hesitate.

From all of the games I watched in the World Cup, there was only one team in the entire tournament that did not do what all the others did. When most players reached the goal with the ball, facing a goal with an open shot, the player stopped, hesitated, and either froze or passed just before taking the shot. The only team that did not do this was the United States. There were forwards like Press who would calculate the odds of making the shot, but she still took the shot- even if it was one in a million. Dutch players hesitated. Japan did too. Had they not, Japan could have won twelve to zero. The final score of the game was 2-1.

After the game, I found the bus back to the hostel immediately. I had grown weary of downtown Vancouver (a year in Sitka will do that to anyone) and settled myself on a crowded bus. In the sardine can that was the public transport, I found myself standing next to a group of high school aged girls in Team USA jerseys. (America, where even at games where we're not playing, we still wear our team's jersey.)

"Were you at the game," I asked knowing the answer.

"Yeah, it was great!" said one of the girls.

"I work at a high school with a lot of the athletes. Do any of you play any sports?" I asked.

"We all play soccer," answered another.

"Who are your favorite players?" I asked.

"Rapinoe," spoke a third proudly.

"Wambach," answered another.

"Morgan," stated a third.

They explained why these were their favorite players. It was because of their athletic records. I told them why I was in town, studying why some girls choose to quit playing sports. They and their parents became interested. I could tell there was a leader among them when she became the spokesperson for the group. "Well I think some girls actually start too early," she said. This intrigued me, so I asked her to explain. "Girls who start when they're three or four lose interest by the time they're our age," she responded. "The best age to start competing is twelve or fourteen. That way, their interest lasts past college."

This last remark hit me pretty hard. I was fifteen when I started fencing, and then I became the lead instructor at a club I started myself in Alaska. I had started my college program too. Most of the athletes I knew in high school are now unhealthy weights and no longer play their sport. "What do you think makes a good team?" I asked. "I compete in fencing. Since it's an individual sport, I don't know a lot about team sports."

"I think," spoke one of the other girls, "It's not about having the best players. It's more important to have a team that works well together."

"A team that communicates well?" I asked.

"Yeah," she replied.

"And a team that doesn't fight," said another girl. She told me a story about how one of their school's rival teams lost almost every game because the team tore itself apart through internal conflict.

"So what breaks a team?" I asked.

"People who play out of position," boldly stated one of the athletes.

Another one explained, "When a player plays someone else's position, it can create conflict among the team."

That was all the information I was able to get from the soccer players before they and their families left the bus. I was able to finally get a seat, and I rode the train until my stop. After walking about fifty feet, I stopped into a pizza-by-the-slice place and wrote down everything I remembered from the conversation. The following day was Wednesday- pub night for the hostels- and I had rebuilt myself from that fateful night the weekend before. As with the previous pub night, the host took us first to *Doolin's*; and I started with a Harp. This time I sat with an Irishman, a New Zealander (aka Kiwi), and a couple of Canadians.

At the first bar, I mostly spoke with the Kiwi- a Maori woman with blue eyes and curly black hair. We spoke about Native Peoples and the issues those in Alaska and New Zealand face today. I told her about my position at the school and my foreign cultures education program. We talked about the film *Whale Rider* and it's plot surrounding the coming-of-age of a girl trying to balance Maori culture with New Zealand (white) culture. I told her how many of my students have similar lives. We got onto the topic of descent practices- matrilineal and patrilineal.

Everything was going well for me- I had already reached my goal of having a great conversation with a well educated person. On our way to the second location, one of the Canadians swooped in while I stepped back to talk to the Irishman. That man knew nothing about matrilineal descent. I felt like the scene in *Toy Story* when Buzz Lightyear sees Sid giving a toy "surgery" and replies, "I don't believe that man has ever attended medical school." I shook off any misogynistic feelings about competing over a woman and moved on to speaking with the Irishman.

I told him the story of me getting escorted out of a faux pub in town. We talked about Irish music before I told him about why I was in Vancouver. Turned out the guy had a lot of positive things to say about women in sports. In fact, he argued that the best Irish Olympian of all time- either male or female- was a female swimmer who had done more for Ireland in the Olympics than any other Irish Olympic athlete. He talked about how much he'd love to see Ireland's women show up in a World Cup. We talked about the Highland Games in Scotland and about how I'd love to write about the women who compete in them.

I found myself on a bus after the fourth bar and headed back to the hostel at one in the morning- four and a half hours after the pub night began. I entered the hostel thirty minutes later, went down to the kitchen to sober up before trying to sleep, and grabbed a cup of coffee from one of the vending machines. There were two other people down there that night at that hour. One, a man from Montreal; and the other, the woman from France who's had to prove herself as a soccer player to sexist dads. I spoke with both of them while sipping my coffee, but the Montreal man left for bed soon after I arrived.

The French woman and I continued to talk about soccer in the empty dining room. She told me she was from Montpellier and told me about what it's like there. I told her about Sitka and what it's like there. Montpellier then told me about the upcoming France v Germany game. She told me about a game back in 1982 between the two men's teams and how Germany defeated France sparking a decades' old rivalry between them. She followed this up with a video of the penalty kick shoot-out that ended the game.

Maybe it was because it was two in the morning, or perhaps because of how passionate Montpellier was about her sport; but as she sat next to me showing videos of France v Germany, a video of Quechua women playing soccer in the Andes, and talking about the 2015 tournament; I had a sobering moment. This feeling was cemented when Montpellier said something I could never forget. She had said how this tournament had become a beacon for hope for girls all over the world that they could not only play sports if they wanted to, but they could be anything they wanted to. The athletes at this tournament were proof.

Montpellier looked me dead in the eyes and announced, "I am proud to be a soccer player. I'm proud to be a woman." I could feel my tattoo again. More importantly, I felt something else. Up to that point, the story had been about me. It had been about my journey into the world of women's soccer. That night- sitting next to that proud soccer player- I knew that's not how it needed to be. I had to tell *her* story. I had to tell the story of women's soccer and after all, I'm not a woman.

"Queen" Loren Gray

The round of sixteen was over by the twenty-fourth. Australia defeated Brazil- to the surprise of many. I watched Japan defeat the Netherlands. England overthrew Norway. Canada pushed through against Switzerland. China dominated Cameroon. The United States *honorably* defeated Colombia. Germany swept past Sweden. France beat South Korea. My bracket was all kinds of messed up. I thought the quarterfinals would involve Cameroon, the United States, Germany, South Korea, Brazil, Japan, Norway, and Canada. Fifty percent wasn't too bad.

On the twenty-fifth, I went to the beach- hippy blanket draped over my shoulders and feet free from the burden of shoes or socks. I read through *Finding the Game* for two or three hours-stopping to take notes in the book's pages. I circled great paragraphs, underlined memorable quotes, and wrote notes to the side of stories that related to my own. Days with no games could be underwhelming.

I would spend most of them at the beach, departing the hostel barefoot with a book in hand. Some days I would walk into Kitsilano's downtown area to check out bookstores and coffee shops. One of the bookstores looked like something out of *Portlandia*. It sold new and used books in half of the store; and in the other half were yoga music cd's, laughing Buddha statues, and self-help manuals with "Gaia, mother goddess" printed over everything.

The restaurants were catered to the local residents- upper middle class to upper class Vancouverites (Oh hey, spell check accepted that word!) with deep pockets. I paid fifteen dollars for a pizza in a small pizza place on one of the main streets. The heat of the sun was melting the inside of the restaurant, and I think I drank twelve gallons of water while waiting for my food to arrive.

When not out of the hostel, I spent most of my time in either the TV room or in the restaurant. There were colorful personalities at both. In the restaurant was the clerk I had spoken to quite frequently. He had graduated with a degree in political science recently and was unsure of what he wanted to do with it. Another man at the restaurant was a chef and part-time clerk. He was under-confident and spoke in what I like to refer to as *half-breaths*.

(This is when everything a person says seems to be on their last ounce of oxygen before exhaling.) The man was a damn fine chef though, and it's something he should be proud of. One of the other chefs/clerks was a woman who seemed to speak English as a second language. She was confident though and took pride in her work. By my last week at the hostel; whenever I walked in and sat down, she brought me coffee knowing it was what I was going to ask for.

The TV room had a regular cast. An Australian (let's call him Brisbane) man and an Australian woman (let's go with Darwin) both worked in the hostel. They frequented the TV room between shifts. Another woman- this one from Nanaimo on Vancouver Island- was an ultimate Frisbee player. Her "brother" who I just have to call *Shark* was an Englishman who was deported to Canada because of some drugs that were discovered on him at an airport.

(I say "brother" because the two treated each other as siblings and *Shark* referred to Nanaimo as his sister on multiple occasions.) There was also Montpellier who showed up during soccer games, a Toronto man who showed up almost everyday to watch baseball, golf, and soccer; and a Brazilian-American who had brought his grandson to Vancouver to watch the World Cup.

When not watching the games, the room was defined mostly by home renovation shows set in Canada. We also occasionally rented movies from the front desk- *a la* "Thelma and Louis". We also watched sports channels, some 90's cartoons, and *Ellen*. The favorite pastime of the room was trying to figure out which channels we could actually watch. (1-29, 80-85, 180-185, 205-230. 92 on Saturdays; 53 on Wednesdays, 34 if you pray very, very hard.) I also napped quite a bit during these days. Without my coffee machine back in Sitka, I was out of my element. I could be found taking a "siesta" almost everyday at around 2pm. Mostly- on my days off- I would take notes on news articles about the tournament.

On the twenty-sixth, *ESPN* was showing the best sports plays of the week. There were clips from the Blue Jays' third baseman making insane catches, but many of the plays featured achievements from the 2015 Women's World Cup. This was the beginning of the pregame show for the most crowded game I watched in that TV room- Germany v France. All forty seats were taken, and ten people stood in the back. Many were French-Canadians, Germans, and anyone else looking to see why there were so many people packed into the room.

Clips from the round of sixteen rolled on the screen, and the line-ups were posted. An Englishman admitted he knew nothing of women's soccer, but still loved watching. When the teams took the field, the national anthems played. French viewers in the room sang their national anthem for the whole room to hear. People made jokes about "sections."

"Oh, you're French?" asked a man in a Bavarian accent. "You guys are over there."

"Yes, yes!" replied a man from Montreal. "This is the winner's section!"

The first half started fast. The French players tested the German goalkeeper- Nadine Angerer- at the one-minute mark. Angerer held her own and made the save. France's offense hammered the Germans who maintained their defense even against free kicks from outside of the goal box. At one point, a referee found herself accidentally saving the ball for Germany. The room made jokes about which jersey she was wearing under her uniform. The first half was dominated by French offense. Germany only made two attempts at the goal during the first half. France's team made twelve.

Neither team scored before the half. At half time, a newsreel of an interview with the US Women's National Team played. One of the German fans remarked that France had great control of the ball but didn't have the power to score when they needed to. The second half began like the first. The French tested Angerer. Germany counter-attacked fast, but France's Necib scored at the sixty-third minute.

At the time of the World Cup, Louisa Necib was twenty-eight and was a major factor for France's success. She played for her country in the U-17, U-19, and U-20 teams and entered the senior competition in 2005 when she was nineteen. My biggest accomplishment at nineteen was finding the perfect recipe for coconut pecan pie. (Thanks Alton Brown!) She played in the 2011 Women's World Cup and the 2012 London Olympics.[51]

For twenty minutes, the game raged on- the ball finding itself on both sides of the field. France made a mistake- a penalty against Germany in the goal box. Germany's Sasic made the penalty kick to tie the game. Celia Sasic retired from soccer after the 2015 World Cup at the age of twenty-seven. She retired with an impressive record. Sasic played for Germany's World Cup team in 2007, 2011, and 2015. She played for the U-20 team in 2004 and 2006, and the Olympic team in 2008- playing in a total of more than twenty international games- excluding friendlies.[52]

At the end of stoppage time, the score was still tied. The game went into overtime, but neither team managed to breach the other's defense. During overtime, a German player elbowed a French player in the face, causing a nosebleed. The athlete came off

---

[51] Lacey. 2015.
[52] FIFA. 2015.

the field, replaced her jersey with a blood-free one, wiped the blood off of her shorts, and ran back onto the field. A German player twisted her ankle, came off the field briefly, and then staggered back on. The German defense and goalkeeper saved four attempted goals. A penalty kick shoot-out would decide the game. Cue Old West music.

Germany made a goal. France made a goal. Germany made a second goal. France made a second goal. Germany made a third. France made a third. Germany sent a fourth into the net. France sent a fourth into the net. Germany made a fifth goal. France's ball landed into the hands of Nadine Angerer. Germany won the game by the last kick of a penalty shoot-out. The next game had me bolting up the stairs to grab my jersey. The United States was going to play China.

During the pregame coverage, the channel showed clips from the US v Colombia game. The sportscasters reminded the audience two American players would be out of the game due to yellow card accumulation (Wambach and Holiday). One of the announcers talked about the US players that would be critical to the US's game. The five anchors talked about Morgan Brian and Alex Morgan first. Then they talked about Amy Rodriguez. Finally, they spoke about China's team before returning to talk about the US just before the commercial break. (America, America, America, China, America!)

The commercials had changed since the beginning of the tournament. They were no longer recycled from the men's competition the year prior. One commercial featured girls of different ages and ethnicities kicking a ball against a brick wall. Eventually, the wall crumbled, and the girls entered a World Cup field. Another commercial featured male and female athletes playing sports including football, basketball, soccer, and baseball.

At the end of the commercial break, the two teams took the field and the national anthems played. Most of the crowd had left. I was in the room with maybe two other people. I didn't care. The United States started the game fast- hitting the Chinese defense hard. China didn't get into the quarterfinals on luck though. The combined effort of their defenders and goalkeeper saved US attempts at the goal at the fourth, nineteenth, twenty-fifth, twenty-sixth, twenty-seventh, and twenty-ninth minute marks.

During the first half, a woman from Portland and I talked about the Portland Thorns- the FC team which featured Tobin Heath, Alex Morgan, Nadine Angerer, and many other athletes who played in the 2015 tournament. China's goalkeeper made another save at the thirty-fourth minute. When someone else in the room remarked about China's skill, I lent my opinion.

"The US is playing to exhaust China's defense," I spoke. "We're not playing to win the half. We're playing to win the game. China's goalkeeper can make fifty saves, but one mistake will give us the win."

China's team survived the first half, but took a pounding. Never once did China take a shot against the US goal. The United States made nine attempts against China. During the half, the people in the room- a growing population- speculated about the England v Canada game. I had a ticket to it. We talked about how epic it would be. There were jokes about which national anthem the Canadian fans would actually sing. Everyone laughed about American football. (It's about the commercials, just admit it.)

Only five minutes into the second half, US's Carli Lloyd scored the first goal of the game. The room began discussing which US player should be substituted in. I thought Sydney Leroux was an obvious choice. After China's goalkeeper caved at the fifty-fourth minute, Kelly O'Hara's nose was bleeding. Like with the French player from the previous game, O'Hara fixed herself up and thrust herself back onto the pitch. Someone in the room said China's government told their team each player would get $250K if they beat the US. I don't know if that was true, but I knew those players weren't getting that money.

During the second half, the room had a lot of discussions- most of them to joke about the Canada v England game. We did however start a conversation about the difference between individual and team sports. I said I prefer playing individual sports because if I lose, I only have myself to blame. If you lose in a team sport, athletes could blame someone else or over-blame themselves and forever believe they let their team down.

Nanaimo jokingly asked, "But who do you get beers with after?"

China's goalkeeper saved again at the seventy-second minute before China finally took the offensive and tested my favorite player.

The US goalkeeper saved at the seventy-ninth minute and the ninety-second minute. The game ended 1-0- US victory. One of the people watching the game was a woman from San Diego who had a job in collegiate women's sports. We discussed the Softball World Series and its popularity among TV viewers. I got to brag about meeting a woman in Sitka who had just graduated from a Minnesota university who played on her school's NCAA softball team.

I went into the hostel restaurant for dinner and sat down with Portland and a Scottish man at the bar. The three of us talked about our travels, about our favorite foods, and about sports. I impressed the Scotsman with my knowledge of Highland Games. After eating and watching a movie with the usual TV room crew, I grabbed *Finding the Game* and headed to the dining room to read.

On Saturday the twenty-seventh, I showered, entered the TV room for a brief viewing, and then headed to catch the bus. A blonde-haired, blue-eyed German woman started talking to me just as we were getting onto the bus. I was about to have a pretty good day. It would not last. "So do you have a ticket to the game?" the German woman asked.

"Yeah, I…" I recollected. "Shit!"

I ran off the bus- leaving behind the beautiful German woman- and ran back to the hostel. I forgot my ticket in my room. After fetching my ticket, I headed back to the bus stop. I made it to the stadium early, so I walked into a pizza-place/coffee shop (Because, yeah, who doesn't want a frappuccino with their calzone?) and found a crowded restaurant. I sat down at a table and welcomed a large group to share space. The group was an extended family visiting from Vancouver Island to watch the game.

Two hundred people from their town came to watch it. This family in particular were huge fans of the Seattle Reign. I asked one of the girls with them who their favorite Canadian player was, and she said Kaylyn Kyle. We talked about how the NWSL (the US national women's soccer league) should televise games because the family- like myself- had to watch games on youtube advertised only on team facebook pages.

After speaking with the family for half an hour, I entered a packed stadium. I would find out later there were nearly fifty-five thousand people in the sixty thousand seat venue. The father-and-daughter duo found their seats and caught the attention of a passing person walking by. She was a former player who was now a field reporter, and she stopped to take a photo with her teenage fan. The three of us Americans sported two 3x5 flags featuring the maple leaf itself.

With Independence Day closing in, I suppose few Americans were going to root for England that day. I saw a photo later that night of San Diego with a giant maple leaf painted over her face. During the line-ups introducing the starting players, the entire stadium echoed with "WHOOOOOOOOOOOO!'s" of celebrating Canada's team. I noticed I was among Americans who were all honorary Canadians that day. During the national anthems, I could hear the audience singing Canada's anthem.

The cheering never flinched when the game transitioned from the pregame to the first half. England started strong. While this is not an excuse for performance, I explain the following because it did in fact play a major factor in the first half of the game. The open-top stadium let in a small ray of sunlight right into the face of McLeod-Canada's goalkeeper- for the entirety of the first half. England's team scored at the eleventh and thirteenth minutes with goals from Taylor and Bronze. A lot of things have to go wrong for a goalkeeper to have to play in a soccer game.

First, a team's forwards have to fail to take control of the ball. Next, the midfielders have to fail to switch to defense, and then the defenders have to fail in their attempt to wrangle the ball from the opposition. If a forward makes a mistake, the score doesn't change. If a midfielder makes a mistake, the score doesn't change. Even if a defender makes a mistake, the worst would be a penalty kick. When a goalkeeper makes a mistake, that's when the opposing team scores. The sun was not helping.

Canada was looking at a definitive loss until Sinclair scored in the fortieth minute. At the half, Canada was down 2-1. During the second half, England's goalkeeper went down when the ball was on the other side of the field. Most people around me were guessing about what it could have been, but I knew. While in college, I took part in a summer archaeology dig on the border of Kentucky and Illinois. This meant that for eight hours a day, five days a week, for four weeks, I worked in 100-degree temperatures digging trenches.

It was horrible. It was rewarding; I was able to experience something I had only one chance to experience. But it was horrible.

We had one participant quit because his body could not endure the weather. Another suffered a bout of heat exhaustion in the kitchen while cleaning dishes- passing out from the heat and hitting his head on the corner of a counter during his fall. A third had to take medications to survive. (Drink more water, people!) When I saw the English goalkeeper fall to her knees and not get up, I knew what it was.

England substituted their goalkeeper out and put a new one in. The game continued. England's forwards kept up their offense. Canada's goalkeeper and defenders made saves at the fifty-fourth, fifty-fifth, sixty-sixth, seventieth, seventy-second, and seventy-fifth minutes. England's defenders saved two attempts at the goal two minutes later. The whole stadium was cheering for Canada. Referee calls were booed by tens of thousands when calls leaned in favor of England's team. England made two more saves before the game ended in an upset. England 2-1 Canada.

As I was exiting the stadium I found myself next to a Canadian man wearing an England jersey exiting with his girlfriend. I want to add that I have zero respect for traitors. I can respect a person who respects other countries. After all, I had just rooted for a Canadian sports team for the last two hours, but to sell out your own country and wear its rival's uniform is cowardly. I already wanted to pummel this pathetic excuse of a human on behalf of Canadians everywhere.

When I heard him answer his girlfriend's question, "So who do you want to win the US/Germany game?" I started thinking about which cave I could dispose of this boy's body in after I depleted it of life.

His answer, "I want to see the US lose."

"You motherfucker!" I thought.

He continued, "Their women are good- *I guess*-- but Germany's just good all around. Plus I hate Americans, apple pie sucks, and my mom can suck a..."

Okay, maybe I invented the last part, but it was the context of what the guy was saying. He thought Germany's women were unbeatable because of Germany's men's record. He was obviously an idiot along with being a traitor. I started thinking about the line from *300*. "Immortals," says Gerard Butler's Leonidas. "We'll put their name to the test." The United States was going to defeat

Germany. We would defeat Germany's team respectfully, and defeat Germany's fans embarrassingly.

I got onto a crowded bus and rode back to the hostel to find new roommates in the co-ed room. The two New Zealanders introduced themselves, and we got to talk about Wonder Woman after the two saw my travel mug. I told them about my blog and how it started. We talked about my study, which led to a conversation about netball. Netball is a sport that evolved similarly to basketball. It is pretty much only played by women- especially professionally- and was for a long time the only televised women's sport in New Zealand.

I left the room with my hippy blanket and headed to the beach. It was already night time- about 11pm, so I left the book at the hostel. As I sat down on a driftwood bench staring out into the harbor, I started thinking about myself. My confidence- I decided- was derived from my passions in life. When I'm at fencing practice, teaching high schoolers about foreign cultures, or writing a new blog post; I'm always at my best. I always feel great when doing these things. When I'm doing none of them, I'm usually pretty down on myself. My confidence plummets. Then I thought that it must be how the soccer players were at this World Cup.

I thought, "If a girl is only confident when she's playing soccer, how destructive must it be if she's not able to play anymore?"

Not just playing sports, but having anything to make a person proud of themselves is essential to happiness. The worst thing that can befall a person- man or woman- is having to give up what they love to earn a living. It was why I refused to earn a degree that would give me a desk job. To this day, I'd still rather be dirt poor than have a desk job. I refused to give up on my goal to become whom I chose to become. On that beach on that night, I decided I was exactly where I wanted to be in life. I felt the athletes competing in the 2015 Women's World Cup shared the same sentiments.

"Back To You" Selena Gomez

The 2015 World Cup was reaching its final stretch. There were four countries left in it- USA, Germany, Japan, and England. On the twenty-eighth, I stopped into the restaurant at the hostel and sat at the bar. Sitting on my left was a man from Perth and to my right was a woman from Quebec City. The three of us all grew up on farms. We talked about what it was like to feed chickens, collect eggs, shear sheep, how goats make the perfect lawn mowers, and the time I had a tie-dyed turkey for a week.

Quebec used to be a rock-climber. She told me she used to climb as often as she could, but had to give it up to get a job and regretted her decision. The clerk spoke with the three of us about US, Canadian, and Australian politics. We all also talked about "settling" in life- when a person settles for a job they aren't crazy about because they are afraid they won't get the career they're actually passionate about. The Australian was able to get a job where he got to travel across the Australian countryside as an employee at a non-for-profit that raised money for charities via bicycle races. He was in Canada for a program his group was starting there. He and I both had gambled on a chance to do something we loved; neither of us regretted our decisions.

Later that night, after watching *Dodgeball* in the TV room, I sat down to read in the dining room. Quebec found me when the only other person had left due to the late hour. She offered me the last of her gin, and- after taking a sip of the vile stuff- I turned down the offer. I told her it was worse than a walrus flipper. (Side note, frozen, fermented walrus flipper is quite possibly the most disgusting thing I have ever eaten.) After talking briefly, Quebec headed out of the dining room and flew home the next day.

I'm going to add here that Quebec looked a lot like Heather Lind. She had shoulder-length black hair and had that French-Canadian accent that would make any American swoon. As an anthropologist on assignment, I had to stick to my ethics on this trip. As a man studying women in sport, it was imperative that I hide every ounce of heterosexuality in my system. There were moments- like in that hostel dining room late at night with Quebec joking with me- where I had to be careful with how I spoke and acted. If there was even a moment that a person in that kind of situation felt uncomfortable, it would have thrown away everything I was trying to learn. I turned down Quebec's gin, and she left the hostel the next morning for home.

On the twenty-ninth, I finished reading *Finding the Game* while sitting on my hippy blanket on the beach. Altogether- and I advise everyone to read it themselves- the book was about four people who chased a dream, refused to surrender to the warnings of their more cautious friends and family, and accomplished the impossible. Later that night, I stopped into the TV room to tire myself out. Inside, I met a twenty-eight year old woman from Miami who'd been playing soccer her entire life.

Miami admitted she prefers playing soccer with men and prefers watching men's soccer. She said women are less likely to play pick-up games. Miami said most of her friends who competed in soccer in high school are now out of shape having quit a long time ago. "I guess with women," she spoke, "when they have a job and get married; they don't get to play sports anymore. Men who have a job and get married go play basketball whenever they want."

Not only was gender/sex playing a major factor in professional sports, it was affecting pick-up games to. According to Miami, it was more socially acceptable for a father to go play soccer with his friends- leaving the family at home- than it was for a woman to do the same. Miami said for this to change, more women's sports need to be televised to show women *can* play sports- even at the pick-up level- just like men could. She also said there needs to be more household names "like LeBron" to inspire more girls to want to play. She also touched on the role of sex appeal, saying a lot of guys care about female athletes because they're hot, not because of their skill.

I told Miami about the book I had just finished reading, a book about four men and women who traveled the world playing pick-up games of soccer. Miami played pick-up games at least once a week in Florida. I told her about the Quechua women in the book, the Palestinian girl, and the women in full hijabs in Iran. I wrote down the name of the book and author at Miami's request, then headed to bed.

When I was growing up outside of St. Louis, I could always tell when a storm was coming. A slate haze appeared on the horizon in the living room window at my mom's house. It would inch its way over the soccer and baseball fields covering the fairgrounds in shadow. The wind would stall, and the trees would freeze as if time had stopped. It was the peaceful pause before a thunderstorm. On Tuesday, 30 June- Vancouver had a similar feel to it.

I had gone down to the TV room with my jersey on. The sports channels were covering Wimbledon. I forgot about tennis, and it was my third favorite sport. I sat down and watched Sloane Stephens win her match before the pregame coverage came on. Two German fans were sitting in front of me paying cards in what looked like a premature victory.

Heather Mitts took control of the table on the television to claim Tobin Heath would be the key to an American victory.

An interview with Nadine Angerer revealed that- like many female players- she had to play with the boys growing up because there were no girls' teams. An interview with Hope Solo revealed her "polarizing" personality. There are few people without strong feelings about the athlete, and she would need to win the World Cup if she wanted to save herself from controversy.

Regardless of the personal lives of either goalkeeper, the game pitted the two best in the world against each other. One of the sportscasters- a former goalkeeper himself- predicted the game would come down to a penalty kick shoot-out, and that he hesitatingly believed Germany would win. Another male anchor blandly spoke about the NWSL before excitedly talking about one male player. Evidently, one man is always more interesting than an entire league's worth of women. The two women at the table- one a former American soccer player and the other a former German soccer player- playfully teased each other about which team would win; keeping things friendly but competitive.

An interview with Abby Wambach followed. She claimed she blamed herself for the 2003 loss against Germany at her first World Cup. Whoever would win the game (USA) it would simply come down to the team that was the best (USA), and the two best goalkeepers in the world (best goalkeeper in the world Hope Solo) would have to prove just how good they were.

When the two teams took the field, there were only two other people in the room with me- *Sie Deutchlanders*. The stadium crew also messed up the US National Anthem- starting the music halfway through the song. "No matter," I thought. "The Germans spent their money on bribes. We spent ours on training our athletes." Another viewer joined before the first half began.

I overheard a German fan after the Germany v France game say, "Alright, now we'll beat the US and head to the final."

I turned around and asked, "Why do you think Germany will beat the US?"

"Oh, I don't know," the German said. "I don't really watch women's soccer. Do you think the US will win?"

"I know they will," I replied calmly.

"Why do you say that?" the man asked.

"I've been studying women's soccer for the past year," I started. "I'm currently writing a book on the World Cup. Germany's good, but they have two or three great players. The US has at least ten." (Apologies, honorable members of the 2015 Women's National Team. We in fact have twenty-three great players, but I was more referring to household names. Please don't hate me.)

When the first half of the game began, more viewers entered the TV room. A sports photographer and the Brazilian-American spoke in Portuguese as they sat next to me. I met the photographer before the Canada v England game. He was an official photographer at the stadium- one of the chosen few allowed to stand closer than the stadium seats and watch the game from five feet away. We had spoken about photographing women's sports before. The Brazilian-American (let's refer to him as NYC because that's where he lived at the time) translated for the photographer.

"He says he prefers photographing women's sports," NYC told me. Angerer saved an attempted goal at the sixth minute mark, pausing the conversation. The two continued to speak in Portuguese. "He says the women are more interesting," NYC resumed. "The men are faster and stronger, but the women are more creative. It makes for excellent photos."

Solo saved at the eight-minute mark. A minute later, Angerer saved. The German offense that started the game ferociously had been stalled. The Americans counter-attacked as the two Portuguese speakers continued talking. The US wrangled control of the ball and dominated its possession. "He says too," NYC continued, "He loves the American fans."

"Really?" I replied- leaning forward to see Brazil chuckling.

"He says he loves the costumes they wear and their enthusiasm," NYC explained. "He says they are the best fans in the world."

My immediate thought, "God damn right!" was less of a thought and more of a spoken outburst.

Well into the second half, NYC and I began talking about Abby Wambach- as she had not started in the game- and about

Coach Ellis. We had both agreed Wambach was best at being a second half substitute. Wambach was excellent at communication and leadership on the field, something critical to a team after the sixtieth minute. Coach Ellis was a genius. She was playing the game to win the World Cup.

For the entirety of the tournament, she was holding her best players back- like war hounds waiting to be unleashed. Team USA was not playing at one hundred percent. To win a game, you play your best every minute. If you do that at a tournament, the teams watching you will know everything you're capable of and will know how to beat you. Ellis was withholding her best plays for the final game. Jill Ellis was in my opinion the most valuable person on Team USA- no contest. She knew how to win a tournament.

By the thirtieth minute, the German advance was stopped. Team USA took the offensive. During a shot at the German goal, Morgan Brian and a German player both went down with head injuries. The German was bleeding at the head. The game paused for seven minutes for medical crews to tend to their injuries. Both players were off the field less than five minutes before heading back onto the pitch.

The German defense saved at the thirty-fifth minute, the thirty-sixth minute, and the forty-third. Both teams displayed professionalism and sportsmanship as they competed honorably. The score was still 0-0 at the half. During half time, NYC told me about his daughter- the mother of the grandson he had brought to Vancouver. (The grandson had flown home the day before.)

His daughter played soccer growing up and still did at the time of the tournament. He was happy to live in a country where that was possible for people like her. We started talking about Sitka- noting how proud I was of the athletes at the high school and those in my fencing program. I wrote down some places worth going to if he ever came to visit. (You're welcome, tourism bureau.)

During the second half, the German player with the bleeding head came onto the field with blood collecting on her bandage. She was still playing- no substitute. Germany's team started the second half strong, but the US were quick to redirect the game towards Germany's goal. Germany's defense saved a goal one minute into the half. Solo was forced to make a save six minutes later.

NYC told me he used to coach boys and girls teams. He preferred coaching the girls. "It's a different game," he said. Angerer saved at the fifty-fifth minute. Solo saved a penalty kick at the sixtieth that went wide. Angerer saved a goal one minute later. "The US can't create enough opportunities," stated NYC. "There's a Portuguese word. *Mah-lee-sia*. I don't know how to describe it in English. It's like… a green banana. The United States are not *ripe* enough to get a goal." The game continued. NYC spoke again. "You might be interested in this. Yesterday, I went out for a walk. Maybe… six in the morning. There was a girl at the field [there was a soccer field right outside of the hostel] practicing drills by herself."

Carli Lloyd scored a goal at the sixty-eight minute mark with a penalty kick. By this time, the room had filled to almost the capacity of the France v Germany game. It wasn't the crown on my mind though, or the goal. It was the story about the girl on the field. I never saw her out there because I never woke up early enough. I did see her in my head though. This was the kind of girl Canada needed to keep in soccer; a person dedicating herself- practicing by herself- to strengthen her skill at a sport she loved. If I remembered correctly, Carli Lloyd said she used to go to soccer fields in New Jersey growing up- playing soccer by herself sometimes- for the love of the game.

Before the end of the game; Kelly O'Hara scored the second goal, and Hope Solo made another save in stoppage time. The United States had defeated Germany 2-0. I paraded into the restaurant in pride that my country had made it to the final game. I ate my dinner to the sound of the post-game coverage before heading to the beach to watch the sunset. Canada celebrates its Independence Day on 1 July.

This however should not be seen how the American Independence Day is celebrated. The United States fought for seven years in a bloody war that saw fighting in cities, on farms, in swamps and mountains. There were campaigns from the Atlantic Ocean to the Mississippi River. America worked its ass off for Independence. No disrespect Canada, but you guys asked the crown for independence and they were like, "Yeah okay. But we still get to design your money."

On 4 July, Americans celebrate independence with fireworks, bbq's, unhealthy amounts of alcohol, apple pie, being awesome, playing baseball, visiting strip clubs, not reading books, losing fingers to explosives, and watching monster truck rallies. Because that's what their Founding Fathers would have wanted. Canada celebrates with beer and fireworks, but not on the first. "We've got work on the second, so we'll party on Canada Day Eve." (More premature celebration in my opinion.) Canadians celebrate Canada Day by overcoming hangovers- celebrating not independence, but simply getting a day off of work. (Independence from work?) *Oh, Canada...*

On Canada Day, 2015, I headed down to the hostel restaurant for coffee, and sat next to an Irishman living in Toronto and an English woman headed to China. She was a metaphysicist- a scientist who studies the physics of the human brain. We talked about what it would take to get more girls interested in becoming scientists. After all; anthropology is a science, and my favorite anthropologist is Margaret Mead.

"More acceptance and encouragement," she claimed.

The Irishman brought up the story of a male Nobel Prize recipient that recently made a sexist comment about women in science labs remarking they were easy on the eyes and insinuated women in science were meant to be things to look at rather than scientists meant to establish breakthroughs and discoveries. I told them about how proud I was to have studied anthropology where- even though sexism still exists- for a large part it is a feminist field where women have been encouraged to participate since Franz Boas' time.

Canada Day that year mattered to *me* because later that day would be the second of the two semi-final games. England would square off against Japan to decide who would lose to the US in the final. Admittedly I had to forgive England's team for not having them on my radar. They had a shot at second place in the tournament, possibly third of they lost to Japan and could beat Germany.

The hostel TV room had the usual cast- NYC, Shark, Toronto, Nanaimo, Montpellier, San Diego, and a bunch of others. It was going to be a great game. We talked about the psychology of athletes. We talked about who we thought would win the game. I said Japan because Japan and England played the same style, but

Japan played it better. We talked about what the US would have to do if they had to play Japan in the final.

"The US will have to score early," I said. "In the first five minutes. Japan plays a disciplined game, but if we can rattle 'em up early on, that discipline will fall apart."

"The US can adapt, eh?" said Toronto. And yes, Toronto spoke like the stereotypical Canadian we Americans love.

"Japan thinks they have set plays for everything," I added. "We have to give them something they're not prepared for." After the two teams took the field, the game began. Japan's defense saved at the fourth minute. England's goalkeeper saved at the sixth. A man from Scarborough said how impressed he was by the pace of the US v Germany game. The current game was going slowly. Neither team impressed me, so I paid more attention to the conversations in the room.

"How big is the field?" Toronto asked. "It's smaller than the men's, eh?"

"I don't know," I answered. "It must be about the size of an American football field though."

"They don't really talk about that do they?" Toronto asked. "The difference in men's and women's game."

I paused to think for the first time about what he was saying. "No," I voiced. "They haven't said anything about it."

"I wonder if that goal's smaller too, eh," Toronto added.

"I can see the goal being shorter," I conceded. "But it's probably as wide as the men's."

"I mean there's nothing wrong with having different sized fields," Toronto continued.

"No, not at all," I said. "And I think it actually makes the game more interesting."

"Less running back and forth and more dribbling, eh?"

"Yeah. The women get to focus more on foot tricks with the smaller field."

Scarborough joined in. "Not to get off subject, but I think this cup will inspire more girls to play in Europe."

"Oh yeah," I replied. "You guys don't really have many clubs for girls over there, do you?"

"We don't have any," he replied. "Girls have to play with boys if they want to play."

"Yeah, I played soccer in grade school in the states," I told him. "We have girls' soccer teams and clubs for girls as young as five; just like the boys."

Japan's Miyama scored against England in the thirty-second minute with a penalty kick. England retaliated with their own penalty kick success. Williams scored at the fortieth minute. After half time, both teams became more interesting. Japan successfully defended three goals at the sixty-first, sixty-third, and sixty-fifth minutes. England saved at the seventy-first.

Japan saved at the eighty-seventh. It looked like it would go to overtime. In stoppage time, one of England's players was following a ball a Japanese player booted toward the goal. Her foot tapped the ball and it went in. Japan won the game because an English defender accidentally scored trying to save the ball. The Japanese players celebrated a victory that in my opinion was not theirs.

After the game, I headed out to Kitsilano to hit up some of the bars. After all, it was Canada Day. I sat down at the bar at my first stop. A man seated next to me pointed to the post-game coverage of the World Cup and told me he prefers golf. I asked him to explain. "I don't know," he said. "I just like it better."

"Do you prefer to watch men or women play?" I asked.

"Women," he said with an answer that surprised me.

"Why is that?" I asked.

"The men can hit the ball farther," he replied, "but the women are usually more accurate. It makes it more interesting to watch." He and I spoke for a while before another joined us, and we continued to talk about women in sports. The two finally left after I got my second beer.

Two more people sat down next to me at the bar. One was another Canadian, and the other an American. He pointed to the post-game coverage showing clips of the US's win against Germany. "I don't like seeing the US win," he said. (Man, some people really hate my country.)

"Why do you say that?" I asked trying to carry myself as a Canadian so I could hear his honest answer.

"The US gloats too much," he answered. It was fair. We do gloat. I gloat. The men and women who compete in American soccer gloat. American football had to introduce a rule against gloating after touchdowns.

"Only the women though," spoke the American.

"You bastard!" I thought.

"The guy continued, "The men don't gloat. Only the women gloat. They should just leave the field quietly after they win." I expected more from my countryman than that. Then again, there's a reason why I felt it necessary to get Wonder Woman's emblem tattooed across my chest. Even when our women are kicking ass and taking names, Americans can still find negative things to say about them.

"It's embarrassing for the country," the American went on.

"Fuck it, I'm ripping this guy's head off!" (Summer mode!)

I didn't say it. I held my tongue back. There are situations I find myself in where I know I would be in danger if I weren't a white male. In one instance, I was in a car with one of my cousins and three of his friends at the University of Virginia. A woman who happened to be African-American forgot to turn her turn signal on before turning. It's something that mildly irritates me- not turning on one's signal. I don't care who does it. The driver of the vehicle I was in started yelling the "N" word. Man was I glad I was white because I thought this southern guy was about to fly up the Confederate battle flag and start singing "Dixieland." It still freaks me out and scares me though.

The incident at the Kitsilano bar made me happy to be a man. When guys start saying clearly sexist things like this guy- especially when they think there's nothing wrong with it- I think about what it would be like to be a woman in the situation. I thought if I tried to speak against his words- as a man- I'd be dragged out into the street and had the shit beaten out of me. I didn't want to think what would happen were I a woman standing up for women against a sexist man.

The two men left as I bought my third beer, begging silently for people that could redeem the previous ones. Two Vancouverites sat down on either side of me. We talked about American and Canadian politics- both individuals portrayed empathy and interest in hearing opinions that contradicted their own. The conservative farmer actually admitted a need for listening to people who think differently and hold opposing opinions- believing a person could only find the truth by triangulating various sources and finding a common story.

We talked about women's hockey, and about the Toronto player who left Canada to play in the US. We also talked about hypersensitivity in regards to political correctness, and I spoke of an article citing Jerry Seinfeld explaining why he doesn't perform at colleges anymore. Since this became a major discussion, I felt it necessary to add my "two cents" about political correctness and comedy.

My favorite movie is *Blazing Saddles*. No movie like it will ever be made again because of the kind of humor presented. There are jokes about Jews, African-Americans, Methodists, Germans, Native Americans, and the Irish. These jokes were not intended to make fun of these people. They were aimed to make fun of people who make fun of these people. This kind of humor can easily be misidentified as racist or xenophobic.

One of my favorite comedians is Chris Rock. He does an incredible job at presenting issues faced by peoples of different races in a way that can make people laugh, but also think and challenge the norm. People in college are taught how to identify racism and sexism and classism and Taoism, and all the other isms; but they're not taught how to talk about them. People I graduated college with still find it uncomfortable to discuss topics related to race, sexuality, gender, and religion. A joke about women- just because it makes a person uncomfortable- does not make it sexist.

I explained to the other two, and the bartender who joined in. "That's what a joke is supposed to do, make people uncomfortable, make people think. A joke about women can be used to illustrate how sexist men can be. It can show how sexist *women* can be."

The great thing about college is that it teaches young adults how to identify issues the world faces today, but it does not teach young adults how to talk about them. At the World Cup, there were clear differences in the men's and women's game. The fields are different sizes. The players are different builds. Just because differences exist, it doesn't mean acknowledging those differences is sexist. The two men finally left the bar after what had been in my opinion the most interesting conversation I had in Vancouver, and it wasn't even about soccer. I left for a second bar, content with the results on the first.

I only stopped into the dark establishment for a single drink. A group of six people hanging out at the bar were talking about who they thought would win the World Cup. 3-3 tie among the six people. I went to the third bar, where I was told I could find a karaoke night. The first song I heard inside was "I'll Make a Man Out of You" from *Mulan*. After singing my own song; I left the loud, crowded bar and headed straight for the beach. It was empty. I loved it. I stood with my feet in the salt water for half an hour before heading back to the hostel.

"Love Myself" Hailee Steinfeld

The next two days seemed infinite as I waited for the next game to take place. People were already forgetting a World Cup was going on. Articles online were showing up featuring the "sexiest" women at the World Cup and replacing the "… but her performance in last night's game…" kinds of articles I had grown to respect. On 2 July, Barcelona told me about how few women play soccer in Spain. It's considered a man's world. There was hope however. Every once in a while, Barcelona said she sees girls playing pick-up games in the streets.

In the TV room, Shark and NYC got into an argument. Shark's personality was blunt. NYC's cordial. They bumped heads when Shark crossed a line when he insulted NYC's accent and his heritage- which he had mistaken his Brazilian heritage for French. When NYC left the room, I told Shark he was being "a bit of a jackass;" and two days later I saw Shark apologizing to NYC for his remarks. NYC and I spoke a lot in those two limbo days. He observed the US play a non-stop, aggressive style of game; but he did not see any signs that Team USA had the ability to change tactics. It would be the latter ability that the team would need to beat Japan. One night, I asked him what he thought of England's loss against Japan- about the final goal.

"What do you think is going to happen when she goes home?" I asked.

"Oh, she'll be fine," he remarked.

"You don't think people will hate her over there?" I asked.

"Those who play soccer won't down her; they won't hate her," NYC explained. "They know mistakes happen. Besides, she was doing it while trying to save the ball. Those who talk bad about her aren't real fans, and their opinion doesn't matter."

NYC had moved to the United States from Brazil. Rumors at the hostel stated he was a retired FIFA referee. Anyone watching a game with him could tell you the first question about every game was, "Did they say where the refs are from?" During games, he would say things like, "Yes, good call," or "No, no, no. Bad call. It should have been…" I don't know if he was ever a FIFA referee, but it didn't matter to me. I learned more about the game from NYC than I did anybody else- including Kansas City.

It was during this window of time I pulled out my laptop to charge and get online to check emails and waste time. After gathering people's names to add to my list of women to spotlight on my blog, I came across a quote from someone on why they consider themselves a feminist and something clicked. I'm the kind of person that when this sort of thing happens, I can't let it go.

I've made fry bread at two in the morning on multiple occasions because I refused to wait until morning to have them. In college, there were more than a dozen times when I walked to the grocery store at three in the morning to buy a dozen donuts. (I swear, this doesn't only happen with fried dough.) I got a coffee from the vending machine and wrote the introduction to this book.

On 3 July, an Australian from Adelaide talked about Australian rules football and our mutual appreciation for the toughness of female soccer players. Any woman that suffers a head injury bad enough to cause bleeding, that throws on a head wrap and runs back onto the field is a-okay in my book. I also gave my contact information to the clerk at the restaurant.
This was probably the tenth time I had wished I'd made business cards. It did not cross my mind people during this study would want to talk to me after I left. In Sitka, I was lucky if I could find another AmeriCorps that wanted to come over for a beer and I considered it a personal victory when one of the employees at my favorite sandwich place in Sitka remembered my name.

I spoke to NYC in the dining room that afternoon about life in Brazil after he spoke with a Brazilian man working at the hostel. He told me they had been talking (in Portuguese) about the worsening state in the country. NYC told me about the government corruption, and how the corruption in FIFA was making things worse. He talked about his neighbors in the US and how he lives among wonderful people. He told me about his home in Mexico- in a small town by the sea. His neighbors there are invaluably friendly, that the food is incredible, and the weather is perfect.

I told him about how much I loved Sitka. "There's five kinds of salmon you can fish, there's halibut and black cod. Herring eggs, oh man," I told him. "And blueberries, and wild mushrooms. Almost everybody has some kind of garden. Everybody who lives there is generous. The weather's rainy, but I kind of like it. It's right at the foot of the mountains where they fall into the ocean." I have a hard time structuring perfect sentences when talking about Sitka. Anyone who lives there understands why. There are just some things words cannot describe.

"And that's what makes you happy," NYC replied to my rant. "It's about the weather, the food, the people. Money can't buy peace." After a pause, NYC asked me what I thought about the final game.

"I think the US will win by a two point lead," I spoke confidently. "Either two to zero or three to one."

"The US plays a fast, aggressive game," NYC repeated. "But they can't change tempo. And Japan should not be underestimated, but if the US makes an early goal..."

That night, I went to the beach to comb through the sand for seashells. I was trying to avoid news about the upcoming games. I walked up and down the beach for two hours collecting violet clamshells the width of three of my fingers. I think I collected over twenty of them. When I returned, I found the TV room filled with the usual crowd plus a man from England who had a soccer ball in his hands.

"Wanna kick around a bit?" he asked me.

I had finished reading *the* book on pick-up games of soccer three days before. I was not about to let the chance to play a game pass me by. "Yeah," I agreed. "Why not?"

The Englishman and I passed across a loose dirt field to the side of the hostel. Dirt flew into the air as we ran side-to-side trying to catch up to the other's passes. It had been the first time since my fencing camp was over that I had been able to actually play anything resembling a sport. I longed to get back to Sitka and have fencing practice again. We finished playing our pick-up game after about an hour, then we went back inside and watched TV.

On 4 July, I threw on my "anthropologist casual" clothes and headed downtown. San Diego had told me about a US Soccer event near the Central hostel in Vancouver that I found myself lucky enough to RSVP for the night before. Due to a misprint on the ticket, I found out I had arrived five hours early. I walked to Doolin's two blocks away to watch the bronze medal game between England and Germany.

I had to stand because there were so many people in the bar- most of them wearing Team USA jerseys. One woman even had her own yellow card she was thrusting into the air every time she thought Germany fouled an English player. Only in Canada during the World Cup will a person ever see an Irish pub full of Americans cheering for English soccer players on Independence Day. At half time, I found a seat at the bar and had a sense of accomplishment come over me as I ordered the usual- Harp in a tall glass. I attempted to talk to the waiting staff before realizing they were insanely busy and didn't have time for my small talk.

I let them be. There was a ritual going on in the pub. New people crowded in- causing a wave like wind blowing through tall grass on the prairie as new people wove their way through trying to find a seat- but also balancing this with finding the ideal location from which to watch the game. In the loud, heavily trafficked pub, I decided any attempt to talk to people would fail. I enjoyed my beer and watched the game. The game raged on over the entire field. Shots were taken on England's goal. Shots were taken on Germany's goal. (Shots were taken on the bar.) At the seventy-fifth minute an English player had a perfect shot, but hesitated. Four times. I could tell she was being overly cautious and that she was over thinking.

"Just take the shot!" screamed the entire pub.

The game went into overtime. A fight near Germany's goal almost erupted. Angerer herself helped the head referee break it up before the German and English players became violent. The almost-fight had come after a German defender fouled an English forward just before she took a shot against Angerer. The English player was given a penalty kick. Williams took the shot and England won the game 1-0. England earned third place. The US fans celebrated as if they themselves had won.

Two women sat down next to me- one from New York City and another from Los Angeles. We talked about my study over a third round of beers as the bar emptied. The two made jokes about how I found the one bar in Vancouver full of lesbians, which led to a conversation about the gay scene in the city. After being there for three weeks, I figured out where the LGBT friendly parts of the city were.

After leaving the bar, I headed to the comic book store where I bought a Wonder Woman book and looked at their action figures. I try to buy female superhero toys when I can. I'm only one person, so I know it doesn't make a difference, but I'm still trying to convince retailers that people really do want to buy action figures of female superheroes- action figures that aren't hyper-sexualized. I bought a Batgirl figure that was pretty awesome.

After stopping into a Starbucks while sitting out the next two hours, I headed to the venue where the pregame party would be held and waited in line. Behind me was a family from Portland. In front of me were two cousins who said their mom was from Belleville- the town I went to high school in. (Small world!) The two cousins- both women- said they played soccer in high school, but had stuck to occasional pick-up games after college.

The mother of the family behind me told me she was forty-two and had played soccer her whole life. She was still playing *futsal* and indoor soccer. (Futsal is a version of indoor soccer where only five people play for each team rather than eleven.) She was in excellent shape and bragged about her two kids who also played the game. While in line; I waved down Nanaimo, Montpellier, and San Diego as they walked by.

When I got inside, I found a table and sat down with my back facing the stage. When the mob had established itself on the dance floor, I noticed a man with a Mia Hamm jersey ten feet away from me. I told the women at the table to watch my action figure and left to find out where the man got his shirt. (My second life goal was to find and own a Mia Hamm jersey that's my size. I still have not achieved this dream. Please buy me one.) I embarrassed myself talking to the man, but found out he got it way back in the 90's in a Nike store.

During the festivities of the evening, I had the nagging feeling I was Aeneas in Troy the day the Trojan Horse was wheeled in. He camped outside the city that night, suspicious of what may have been inside the horse. People should have listened to that guy. (Did I mention I grew up reading books on mythology?) "I'll celebrate when I know we've won." I thought as people around me got drunk off premature victory.

I pulled a torn out newspaper page from my jacket pocket. I found it in Starbucks while I was wasting time, but didn't have time to read it in the coffee shop. While the other folks from the hostel enjoyed their evening on the dance floor, I pulled out my pen and took notes on the article. Carrie Serwetnyk from the Vancouver Sun wrote that the US would need to rely on Jill Ellis and Carli Lloyd to win the final game. She also wrote that the US played an aggressive game while Japan played safe.[53] Matthew Robinson wrote about the high demand for tickets to the game and that US fans would be swarming to the stadium in both numbers and enthusiasm.[54]

By 9:30, most of the families had left the event- leaving only those in college and recently graduated behind. I couldn't help but think what the previous Women's World Cup pregame party was like- if there even was one. This World Cup was the beginning of a new era for women's soccer- one where people waited for hours to get into a pregame party. Premature celebrations aside, I was proud to be witnessing first hand a moment of history.

I thought of a quote from my favorite Shakespeare play. It's a prologue where the chorus begs the crowd to forgive Shakespeare for the "unworthy stage" they were using to put on a show of such grand history and scale that only the audience's collective imagination could allow the theatre to tell the story.

O for a Muse of fire, that would ascend
The brightest heaven of invention,
A kingdom for a stage, princes to act
And monarchs to behold the swelling scene!
Then should the warlike Harry, like himself,
Assume the port of Mars; and at his heels,
Leash'd in like hounds, should famine, sword and fire
Crouch for employment. But pardon, and gentles all,

---

[53] Serwetnyk. 2015.
[54] Robinson. 2015.

The flat unraised spirits that have dared
On this unworthy scaffold to bring forth
So great an object: can this cockpit hold
The vasty fields of France? or may we cram
Within this wooden O the very casques
That did affright the air at Agincourt?
O, pardon! since a crooked figure may
Attest in little place a million;
And let us, ciphers to this great accompt,
On your imaginary forces work.
Suppose within the girdle of these walls
Are now confined two mighty monarchies,
Whose high upreared and abutting fronts
The perilous narrow ocean parts asunder:
Piece out our imperfections with your thoughts;
Into a thousand parts divide one man,
And make imaginary puissance;
Think when we talk of horses, that you see them
Printing their proud hoofs i' the receiving earth;
For 'tis your thoughts that now must deck our kings,
Carry them here and there; jumping o'er times,
Turning the accomplishment of many years
Into an hour-glass: for the which supply,
Admit me Chorus to this history;
Who prologue-like your humble patience pray,
Gently to hear, kindly to judge, our play.
Henry V: Prologue
William Shakespeare[55]

For some athletes, as much as forty years went into preparation for this tournament. Forty years of the fight for a girl's right to play sports at school in the United States had paved a path of opportunity. Twenty-three women, some who had never competed in a World Cup before, others who would be competing in their last were about to meet their rival team. Japan defeated the United States in the 2011 World Cup. The United States defeated Japan in the 2012 Olympics.

---

[55] Shakespeare. 1559.

Both teams were aching for the final trophy. These two teams- forged literally from years of blood, sweat, and tears- were about to square off at the most important sporting event in the history of women's soccer. The stadium was built for a different sport altogether. The grass was made from blades of plastic. And a man with only a bachelor's degree in anthropology and only a Wonder Woman themed blog to back his experience in feminist studies was recording the tale.

By all means, I shouldn't have even been in Vancouver. A month before I met the Olympian that visited my university's fencing club; I received an email from the job I trained for the past four years to get. It was a teaching position for an organization similar to AmeriCorps. The email read that they would not accept my service. For a week, I kept it a secret. I wanted to make a new plan before I told anybody what had happened. When I met the Olympian, she started the seminar by explaining how important it is to set goals.

"Even if it's as simple as 'I'm going to do my laundry today', you have to set goals." After the seminar, while the Vice President of the club and I drove Nicole Ross to the airport, I decided I wanted a job where I could inspire young girls to keep playing the sports they love. I applied for the Peace Corps.

The interviewer asked how I would respond to culture shock, "For instance, if you see that a girl can't play soccer because it's what boys do."
I replied, "I understand that the culture is different from the US, but keeping women from making their own choices has nothing to do with culture. I'd make the boys play soccer with that girl."

"That's exactly what I wanted to hear," my interviewer admitted.

I actually received the position. But, I turned it down. I took a chance on an offer my sister gave me and moved to Alaska. Had I been accepted into the teaching program, had I not met the Olympian, had I gone to Costa Rica; had I done any of those things, I wouldn't have been in Vancouver on the eve of the final game with a ticket in my backpack.

I am now pulling a Deadpool and speaking directly to you, the reader. I wish I had a doctorate in anthropology. I wish I could say I was a professional anthropologist. I didn't and I wasn't. (I didn't even have business cards.) I was a professional volunteer and I worked with high schoolers in a small, Alaskan town. I was the least qualified person to write this book, but I was what you got. With that being said, excuse my imperfections. Excuse my lack of experience. This book is not about me. This book is about Carli Lloyd and Megan Rapinoe.

This book is about Vero Bouquette and Nadine Angerer. It's about the woman from Montpellier that had to prove herself to sexist fathers, the woman from Barcelona that grew up in a culture where only boys got to play soccer. This is about the mom from Portland that keeps playing, the dad from Kansas City that brought his daughter to witness a sport she loves. This book isn't just about women playing soccer; it's about everything that had to happen, that *has* to happen, behind the goal to make this sport universal.

Chapter 5: Stoppage Time

"Thunder" Leona Lewis

I woke up on 5 July to an orange sky peeping into the window. Wildfires were raging north of the city and on Vancouver Island. Smoke from both fires was blowing over the city. I left the hostel for the bus stop at noon. I made sure not to forget my ticket that time. I also made sure to dress the part. The half-buttoned anthropologist was no more. I had dressed myself to resemble a member of the Continental Army during the American Revolution: boots, knee-high socks, fencing knickerbockers, gray dress shirt, blue and red coat. I turned heads at the bus stop.

I met a group of Portlanders on the bus and talked about my study. One of the family members told me she competed in track & field and told me a story about how that year at the NCAA track & field nationals, officials segregated the men's and women's events because the men were going to be televised. Before, men and women competed simultaneously.
I competed in track & field in grade school. During running events, boys and girls competed side-by-side. It helped save time and was- of course- not sexist. Another member of the Portland family told me she still played, her daughter played, and her husband was a coach for a girls' team. (Portland, Oregon; you folks are doing things right over there!)

After getting off the bus, I found myself in the same frapacalzone place I was at before the last game. I had a pizza, then left to enter the stadium. After weaving my way through the stadium, I sat down in my seat three hours before the game started. The stadium had sent emails to ticket holders telling them to get seats early. I followed their advice. The TV screen above the field displayed video clips from former Women's World Cups before showing highlights of the 2015 tournament. Fans arriving at the game early took photos near me. My seat wasn't behind the goal this time. It was about twelve rows from the bottom, on the sidelines where I could see the entire game play out.

I saw girls using US flags as *lava-lavas*. (Wraps worn like skirts in Pacific Island nations) They were the US soccer players I met on the crowded bus returning from the Netherlands v Japan game. The TV screen showed every goal scored to date at the 2015 World Cup next as the stadium crews watered the field. Some of the players entered the field to warm up. Chanting for the US began. Smoke was falling from the sky- filling the stadium in a haze as the sky above the stadium became transitioned from blue to gray.

The father and daughter from Kansas City arrived and sat down next to me. I adopted the concept of a flag cape, unfurled my stars and stripes over my shoulders, and tied the corners. A man four rows in front of me had an American flag painted on his bald spot. Seated to the right of me were two soccer players from New York. They played their whole lives including intramural in college. Vice President Joe Biden found his seat. He was two hundred feet away from me.

The line-ups arrived on the TV screen, and the announcer introduced the players. The flags paraded onto the field with starting players in tow. During the US National Anthem, I sang along with every American fan at the game. (I don't know how many of us were there. The stadium had fifty-four thousand attendees that day. I guess some of them were Japan fans.) The Japanese fan drummers sounded their instruments, and the game began.

I didn't even have time to sit down. At two minutes and thirty seconds, Carli Lloyd scored a corner kick. The entire stadium stood to watch. All American fans erupted in noise. Just when I sat down again, Carli Lloyd scored again at the fifth minute with a free kick. "Man," I said to Kansas City. "I'm not going to be able to sit down."

By the fifth minute, I had already lost my voice. Japan counterattacked, but Solo saved the ball at the twelfth minute, then Lauren Holiday scored a minute later. Japan's players were all kinds of riled up. Carli Lloyd rocketed a ball- with her back foot on the mid-field line- over the head of Japan's goalkeeper right into the goal. I thought the stadium was going to riot. At the fifteen-minute mark, the score was already three to zero.

Japan stepped up their game and finally put one past Hope Solo at the twenty-seventh minute. The American defense and Solo saved two attempted goals two minutes later. I once joked that if Japan's fans' instrument was a drum, the Americans' would be "Booing" referee calls. This became true. I thought the American fans were going to storm the field and burn the referees like witches.

The US team slowed down leading up to the end of the half making one more shot at Japan's goal at the forty-first minute.

The American offense came back in full throttle when the second half started. The Japanese had to make saves at the forty-eighth and forty-ninth minutes. In a repeat from the England v Japan game, an American defender trying to save the ball accidentally put it into the goal. Japan had their second point because of someone on the opposing team. The United States was keen to wash away any chance of a Japanese victory. Two minutes later, Tobin Heath scored.

The game turned to the goalkeepers. Solo made saves at the sixty-seventh minute, the seventieth minute, the seventy-third minute, the seventy-fifth minute and the eightieth minute. Ellis threw Abby Wambach and Christie Rampone onto the field. It would be their last World Cup. United States defenders saved at the eighty-eighth. Japan's goalkeeper saved at the ninetieth. Solo saved in stoppage time. The United States had just won the 2015 FIFA Women's World Cup 5-2 against Japan.

Both teams were in tears. While the stadium crew brought out the awards ceremony stage, Wambach retreated to the sidelines to embrace her wife with tears. Team USA draped each other in American flags. Sydney Leroux repeated Wambach's move with her husband. During the awards ceremony, awards for individual athletes were announced. Hope Solo earned her second Golden Glove. Carli Lloyd earned the Golden Ball. Japan earned their second place finish. The whole stadium cheered as they collected their trophies. The stadium erupted as the US collected theirs.

After the confetti cannons switched on, Japan's team retreated to their locker rooms. Team USA's families entered the field. Mothers on the team brought their children onto the field. There was a five-year-old bathing in confetti. Ellis and her family took photos at the podium. The fans were celebrating, the team was celebrating, and toddlers were running around on the field.

People asked me a lot what it was like to be at the game. To be completely honest, I still cannot answer that question. It was a moment of history. There was queasiness in my gut. Every song played became a trigger for memories. There were tears involved. There was just a moment when- and I know this is so cliché- time seemed to just not exist. For one moment I was in some special bubble in the space-time continuum where I had experienced a lifetime of emotions in two hours. It's a feeling a person can only understand if they've experienced it. The bubble had to end at some point though.

"That's it," I whispered to myself. "It's time to go."

I folded up my flag, grabbed my trash, and left my seat leaving the field behind me. When I exited the stadium, the smoke had become thick. Vancouver looked like Beijing. On a normal day in the street Doolin's occupied, a person could look across a bridge that led to Kitsilano. That day, I couldn't even see the bridge. It was maybe two miles away, and completely invisible.

I found an empty table at the bar and ordered a Harp. (I'm predictable.) I invited two American fans to sit down when all other tables were occupied. One was from Philadelphia and the other was from Portland. All three of us were in awe after the game. We talked about Johnston and Krieger; Lloyd, Solo, and Rapinoe; Rampone and Wambach. None of us spoke in coherent sentences. I told them I was an AmeriCorps. They told me they were Jesuit Volunteers (a sub-organization within AmeriCorps). The game was replayed on the television screen above us. We made jokes about betting on the game.

I took a bus back to the hostel after drinking, eating, and having a brownie a la mode. I spent fifty bucks at the pub that night-not a loonie regretted. It was getting dark. By the time I had finished reliving the game with Shark and NYC, it was late and I decided to head to bed. There were people outside talking about the game, and I heard a familiar voice.

I left the bed and headed outside to find Montpellier talking to two Frenchmen. She invited me to walk to the beach with her. Neither one of us could sleep. Montpellier sat down on a driftwood bench. I sat down in the sand. We talked about the game we had both witnessed. We talked about how important the tournament had been to girls all over the world.

"And the children on the field," Montpellier opened. "The moms brought their kids on the field. Those kids' moms just won the World Cup. They're like supermoms!"

We sat at the beach until one in the morning talking about the World Cup. We talked about how the two of us ended up there. We talked about our family and friends who receive more praise from their parents and grandparents. I told her about how I cope with hearing stories of my relatives that are the favorites in my family. (Professional volunteer is not high up on the hierarchy of my siblings/cousins' careers. I can bake one hell of a red velvet cake though, and I once ate twelve donuts in one sitting. My self-confidence is impregnable.)

She said, "A person has to do things for themselves. It sounds selfish, but it's true. If you do things to get approval from others, you'll never be happy. Nobody can have everybody like them. But if you do things for yourself- even if people hate you- at least you can feel good about yourself."

My thoughts exactly. I adhere to the *Irish Goodbye*. When Montpellier and I entered the hostel, she said, "Goodnight," and I said "See ya later," as casually as I always do. And that was it. I felt horrible about five minutes later. It was the last time I saw Montpellier. As I laid down in my bed, I thought about everything I should have said to her and everyone else I would never see again before finally falling asleep after the most eventful day of my entire life.

The next day; I checked out of my room, called a cab, and headed for the airport. There was a dream-like sense to all of it. I lived in Vancouver for three weeks. I woke up, checked out of my hostel, and entered a cab in the time span of less than an hour. I looked back more than a hundred times during that cab ride. As we were driving, I saw NYC playing tennis with his wife.

I wanted to jump out of the cab to say goodbye to him- feeling regrets from my embarrassingly rude parting the night before. As I made my way through airport security (Yes, my hair has grown a foot since I got my passport photo. No I do not have plums this time.) and found my seat on the airplane, I couldn't help but replay the last three weeks in my head. I was heading home, leaving behind not only the game, but also an entire world, behind me.

"A Love Song" Ladyhawke

On the plane to Seattle, I made a mistake talking about my study. The American fans seated facing me on the plane had no respect for my favorite player. They called her a "terrible role model," and I thought I was going to be thrown out of the plane trying to defend her. Less than twenty-four hours following the US victory, the United States was back at character destruction and denial of agency.

(Character destruction is when a person or people attack a person's personal life as a means of diminishing any career achievements. Denial of agency is any time a person or people use any means to refuse to admit the achievements of another person.) This did not surprise me. I withdrew from the topic and stared out of the window for the entirety of the flight.

"I guess I have more books to write," I thought, trying to put a positive twist on the subject. "I think I should write about rodeos next summer."

After arriving in Seattle, I met a familiar face. One of the councilors at the high school was returning from Portland, Oregon. She offered me one of her Voodoo donuts as we talked about my trip. I was sad about leaving Vancouver, but it was nice to see someone familiar. A little piece of Sitka had welcomed me in Seattle. The second plane stopped in Ketchikan to pick up passengers. A dozen Native Alaskans boarded.

"I'm definitely back in Alaska," I thought. It was going to be good to be home.

Before I left the hostel that morning, I asked my sister if she could pick me up at the airport. When I stepped off the plane, I had a pain south of my stomach. I needed to use the bathroom. When I entered the lobby of the airport in Sitka, I saw a horde of Wilsons standing in front of me. My grandma and five of my cousins had arrived two days before for a weeklong visit.

They greeted me with a sign that read, "World Cup Anthropologist."

I dropped my bags in front of them and greeted them with, "I gotta pee. Watch my shit."

After relieving myself in the bathroom, I returned to them exhausted. It took me a few days to get back into my old habits. I went back to house sitting. I drove to the house my family was renting when I could. My brother and his girlfriend joined us the day after I got back. My cousins teased me with questions about the final game.

"So what was the score after six minutes?"

"What was the score at the half?"

"What was the score after eight minutes?"

"Who scored the fourth goal?"

"What was the score after three minutes?"

I answered every question accurately. The most difficult part of returning to Sitka was the free time. I had a lot of it. I lived in a house with five roommates. None of them ever seemed to be around during the day. (What, do they have jobs or something? How lame.) At the hostel, there were always people around. I had to leave the house to do anything. I'd hang out with my family when I could, but there were nights where sleeping in an empty house seemed lonesome. I watched a four-season TV show on Netflix in three days.

I ran into another high school employee while at lunch one day. He had grown his beard out. I barely recognized him. "Boy," he told me, "You picked the right game to go to." I just laughed. He was right. I picked the right game to go to.

Epilogue

"Clearest Blue" CHVRCHES

In December of 2015, Abby Wambach retired from soccer and wrote her memoirs, which included the tale of her struggles as a drug addict while trying to balance recovery with athletic training. After retiring from soccer, Wambach continued to help push for equal pay. Amy Rodriguez sat out the 2016 Olympics with her new title as a two-time mother. The veteran forward planned to return to international duty after the birth of her child, but- as of 2017- the 2015 team member remained on the proverbial bench of the USWNT.

Christen Press- one of the rookies for the USWNT in 2015 became a deciding factor in the 2017 USWNT's games. Not only did her skill improve, but also Press became one of three team members elected to serve as the USWNT representatives. After the 2016 National Women's Soccer League (NWSL) season, Alex Morgan signed onto a European soccer club and left her Florida team to play in France. Forward Sydney Leroux also sat out the 2016 Olympics to become a mother. Leroux gave birth to her son in September and- shortly after- made plans to return to soccer.

After the 2015 World Cup, midfielder Shannon Boxx retired from international soccer duty as a champion footballer. Another rookie on the 2015 team, Morgan Brian became a seasoned veteran by the 2017 international season. The midfielder became stable pillar for the USWNT. After finishing the World Cup as a strong veteran of the international team, Tobin Heath continued to shine as a US midfielder well into 2016. In December, Heath was named the US Soccer Female Player of the Year and continued to play with the international team.

After the 2015 World Cup, Lauren Holiday was forced into early retirement. Suffering symptoms of a brain tumor, the retired soccer star had to deal with the repercussions from giving birth to her child and having brain surgery in the same twelve-month window of time. Still in recovery, Holiday continued to struggle with her post-surgery life. Carli Lloyd remained a lead member of the USWNT, but doubled as one of five team members suing US Soccer for pay inequality.

Veteran midfielder Heather O'Reilly also retired from international duty following the 2015 World Cup, but continued to play in the club leagues. In 2017, O'Reilly announced she signed with the English women's Arsenal club and that she would be leaving the NWSL. Midfielder Megan Rapinoe responded to racial injustice after the World Cup by protesting national anthems at games. The move caused stirs in the soccer world and- along with a minor injury- led to Rapinoe being excluded from the international roster for the 2016/17 international season.

Becky Sauerbrunn, became a captain of the USWNT and served alongside teammates Christen Press and Meghan Klingenberg as team representatives. Christie Rampone was the last player on the USWNT who had served since the birth of women's international soccer and retired in 2017 after a lifelong career of leading the team through failure and success. Dubbed "Captain America" by her teammates, Rampone retired as a veteran soccer player to one of the greatest groups of women to play at the World Cup.

Kelley O'Hara remained a central player in the USWNT after the World Cup and served on the team for the 2016 Olympics. O'Hara remained a staple of the international team. In 2016, Ali Krieger- still a major defender for international duty- learned that her team traded her in the NWSL. The move exposed tension among the NWSL community, which had issues with athletes' rights in the 2016 season. While Krieger herself did not make comments about the trade, she was part of a larger group of women who protested the new rule in US Soccer regarding protests against the National Anthem.

Meghan Klingenberg also remained a vital defender in the USWNT after her rookie appearance in the 2015 tournament. Klingenberg served alongside teammates Press and Sauerbrunn as team representatives. Julie Johnston returned from the World Cup a star player for the international roster and continued to serve the team in the 2016 Olympics. Johnston continued to play for the international team and for her NWSL club in Chicago after marriage changed her name to Julie Ertz.

In 2016, her head coach released Whitney Engen- who had served on the USWNT since 2010- from service. The emotional end to her international service led to Engen stepping away from soccer entirely when in 2017 she announced she would be retiring from club soccer. After the 2015 World Cup, Lori Chalupny also retired quietly from soccer. The athlete had briefly resumed soccer duty in 2015 after retiring to coach status in her hometown.

Goalkeeper Ashlyn Harris was one of two top picks after Hope Solo's self-exile from the team. Harris received no game time during the 2015 World Cup, but her experience in the NWSL as the lead goalkeeper for the new Florida team (Orlando Pride) proved her worth as a goalkeeper. Alyssa Naeher also served as a relief goalkeeper in 2015 and played the part as head goaltender during the 2017 SheBelieves tournament.

Hope Solo continued to bat away controversial headlines after the 2015 World Cup, but managed to turn those headlines into articles about her and her teammate's fight for equal pay in their lawsuit against US Soccer. After her failed performance at the 2016 Olympics and for rude comments made toward the team that beat the US, Solo received word that US Soccer was suspending her for unsportsmanlike conduct.

The move was heralded as an outdated decision, which should have been made earlier, though equally considered overly harsh. Solo took it upon herself to take a voluntary leave of absence from club duty with the Seattle Reign. The goalkeeper's suspension ended just before the SheBelieves Cup in 2017, but the athlete remained off of the international roster.

The roster for the US international team for 2017 included a plethora of fresh rookies and resembled the 2015 team loosely. Forwards included two veteran forwards (Alex Morgan, and Christen Press) and four rookies (Crystal Dunn, Jessica McDonald, Mallory Pugh, and Lynn Williams). The team fielded three returning midfielders (Carli Lloyd, Tobin Heath, and Morgan Brian) along with five new midfielders (Brianna Pinto, Samantha Mewis, Allie Long, Rose Lavelle, and Lindsey Horan).

There were four returning defenders (Becky Sauerbrunn, Kelley O'Hara, Ali Krieger, and Julie Johnston) and two new defenders (Casey Short and Emily Sonnett). The goalkeeper roster included returning players Alyssa Naeher and Ashlyn Harris along with new goalkeeper Jane Campbell. The 2015 US Women's National Team (USWNT) won the gold medal after taking first place in the FIFA World Cup that summer; and were heralded home by parades, late night show interviews, and a meeting with their nation's president.

Members of the team formed a five-person committee for suing for the right to equal pay. But not all of the team's players returned to the roster for the Olympic tournament the following year. In 2016, the US team finished with a record low in an international championship and was the first time in the team's history where they finished lower than third overall.

"Sue Me" Sabrina Carpenter

The players of the USWNT expected to finish at least third in the Rio Olympics, and were planning on using their finish as a platform for the final stage of achieving pay equality. Because of their record low finish, progress fell backwards tremendously. Almost overnight, US audiences seemed to almost completely forget about women's soccer. Over the next two years, the players of the USWNT scrambled to readjust to respond to growing talent across the world.

Perhaps Tosh.0's joke about the US women being as good as they were because of little competition abroad was right. The US men's soccer team consists of great players, but it's hard for them to compete against men that have been playing the game for generations. English men literally invented the game of soccer (in the Middle Ages!). US women however pretty much invented the women's game.

After the 2015 Women's World Cup, international audiences of women and girls paid attention and started playing soccer in tremendous numbers. That shift led to other countries increasing the skill of their women's national teams. Sweden defeated the US in the 2016 Olympics to prevent the US from earning any medals in the tournament, then France and England were defeating the US in minor tournaments over the next two years. Australia's team was quickly improving as well and countries where women would never be allowed to wear shorts in public were starting to make headlines for their women's soccer teams- including Afghanistan and Jordan.

The USWNT had to reclaim their throne in 2019's Women's World Cup. The team carved through the competition and regained their "top of the world" status with a gold medal finish. The players were able to start negotiating for new pay with US soccer- which as of 2019 was still not equal. Other countries were expanding their quality past single players- especially Spain and Brazil. In the NWSL, viewership skyrocketed. Teams were getting unprecedented attendance at games.

"Makes Me Wonder" Ella Mai

After five years of writing about women's sports, people often ask me why an anthropologist feels sport is an important topic for research. I usually use the example of the 2015 World Cup for why. Sports can often elevate cultural topics to a public platform. In the case of the United States, women still earn less pay than their male counterparts in several industries- even though there are laws banning unequal pay on the basis of sex.

US Soccer is an employer that employs male and female soccer players, but pays them differently. This inequality is likely to not end soon. While the US men's soccer team does not get as many viewers as the US women, men's sports definitely get more viewership than women's. On major sports networks aired in US televisions, there are usually men's sports numbering in the double digits, but few- if any- women's sports aired.

It's not easy finding women's sports leagues and athletes to watch with the flooding of men's sports on television. ESPN's flagship channel includes men's American football, soccer, basketball, baseball, tennis, and hockey (among others) while their only regularly aired professional women's sports were tennis and basketball. That being said, there are several women's sports across the world that are easy to watch, and just as entertaining as men's sports.

Both of ESPN's televised professional women's sports are definitely worth watching. Women's tennis players are actually (usually) the highest paid women athletes in the world- and for good reason. The easiest events to watch are the Grand Slam tournaments- the Australian Open, the French Open, the US Open, and Wimbledon. Viewers can find all of these events aired on ESPN. The US women's basketball league- the WNBA- also is definitely worth watching. (I even wrote a book about it- *Behind the Basket* by Joseph C Wilson).

NWSL soccer is rapidly becoming the epicenter of women's club soccer around the world as the league heads into the 2020 season with expansion on their horizon. I wrote a book about the Seattle team in 2018- *Behind the Goal 2*. Another great professional league is the ANZ Premiership- a netball league in New Zealand. Netball is similar to basketball; but there is no dribbling, no traveling with the ball, and no backboard on the net. Viewers outside of New Zealand can watch games for free on the league's website aired live.

The World Surf League is also a definite watch. Women surfers have made waves (get it?!) for years as equals to their male counterparts on the waves of the world. In 2019, the league announced it would pay their men and women athletes equal for the first time in history. Viewers can catch live Championship Tour (similar to tennis' Grand Slam series) tournaments on the league's website. (You can also read about surfing with my book *Behind the Break*.)

Several college sports are also worth watching. Softball is probably the most viewed collegiate women's sport, followed shortly by indoor volleyball. Basketball and soccer are also both worth watching. For live games, my favorite sport is actually roller derby. Almost every community in the US has a local team, so viewers wanting to support local, grassroots women's sports can watch their local roller derby team.

It's hard to say what the future holds for women's sports- and that's not necessarily what anthropologists are supposed to do. What I can say after five years is that there has been significant change in sports involving a mass opening of opportunities for women across the world and across sports. More women than ever are playing sports in the Twenty-First Century, and that will likely not change anytime soon.

In the event that any anthropologist, potential sponsor, badass athlete, or family member who's forgotten my contact information is interested in getting in contact with me; please do! I would love to talk women's sports, feminist anthropology, Wonder Woman comics, favorite flavors of ice cream, etc with all of you! Please send an email to josephwilsonanthro@gmail.com.

"Small Talk." Katy Perry. *Small Talk*. Capital Records. 2019.

"My Life." Chloe Jane. *My Life*. Chloe James. 2017.

"Love and Run." Lexie Liu. *2030*. 12 Tone Music. 2019.

"Inside Out." Camila Cabello. *Camila*. Epic Records. 2018.

"Issues." Julia Michaels. *Nervous System*. Republic Records. 2017.

"Confident." Demi Levato. *Confident*. Hollywood Records. 2015.

"I'll Be There." Jess Glyne. *Always In Between (Deluxe)*. Atlantic Records. 2018.

"Whole Wide World." Mindy Gledhill. *Anchor*. Mindy Gledhill. 2010.

"Dangerous Woman." Ariana Grande. *Dangerous Woman*. Republic Records. 2016.

"Lush Life." Zara Larsson. *So Good*. Epic Records. 2017.

"Road Less Traveled." Lauren Alaina. *Road Less Traveled*. 19 Recordings. 2017.

"New Rules." Dua Lipa. *Dua Lipa (Deluxe)*. Dua Lipa Limited. 2017.

"Drinkee." Sofi Tukker. *Drinkee*. HeavyRoc Records. 2015.

"You Need To Calm Down." Taylor Swift. *You Need To Calm Down*. Taylor Swift. 2019.

"Level Up." Ciara. *Level Up*. Ciara Universal Music Publishing. 2018.

"Queen." Loren Gray. *Queen*. UMG Recordings. 2018.

"Back To You." Selena Gomez. *13 Reasons Why (Season 2)*. Interscope Records. 2018.

"Love Myself." Hailee Steinfeld. *HAIZ*. Republic Records. 2016.

"Thunder." Leona Lewis. *I Am*. Island Records. 2015.

"A Love Song." Ladyhawke. *Wild Things*. Polyvinyl Records. 2016.

"Clearest Blue. CHVCHES. *Clearest Blue*. Glassnote Entertainment. 2015.

"Sue Me." Sabrina Carpenter. *Singular Act I*. Hollywood Records. 2018.

"Makes Me Wonder." Ella Mai. *READY*. 10 Summers Records. 2017.

Works Cited

"Abby Wambach." Biography.com. A&E Entertainment; 2015.
"About." Lisa De Vanna: The official site of Lisa De Vanna. 2015.
"Alex Morgan." Biography.com. A&E Entertainment; 2015.
"Alex Morgan fulfills European ambition by joining Lyon."
ESPNW. Associated Press; 7 January 2017.
"Ali Krieger's Story- One Nation. One Team. 23 Stories." One
Nation One Team. US Soccer; 2015.
"Alyssa Naer's Story- One Nation. One Team. 23 Stories." One
Nation One Team. US Soccer; 2015.
"Amy Rodriguez' Story- One Nation. One Team. 23 Stories." One
Nation One Team. US Soccer; 2015.
"Ashlyn Harris' Story- One Nation. One Team. 23 Stories." One
Nation One Team. US Soccer; 2015.
"Becky Sauerbrunn's Story- One Nation. One Team. 23 Stories."
One Nation One Team. US Soccer; 2015.
Blake, Paul. "Fifa scandal: Why the US is policing a global game."
BBC News Online. BBC News; 28 May 2015.
Boehm, Charles. "Soccer power couple Dom Sawyer, Sydney
Leroux welcome new son Cassius Cruz." MLS Soccer; 12
September 2016.
Borden, Sam. "Abby Wambach, Retired US Soccer Star, Reflects on
Her Addiction." The New York Times; 10 October 2016.
Boren, Cindy. "Hope Solo's half-sister, new documents reveal ugly
details of domestic violence incident." Washington Post Online. The
Washington Post; June 2015.
Brown, Kayan. "She's a Girl, So What?." Women's Sports
Foundation; 7 October 2008.
"Carli Lloyd Biography." Biography.com A&E Television; 8 March
2017.
"Carli Lloyd's Story- One Nation. One Team. 23 Stories." One
Nation One Team. US Soccer; 2015.
"Cartwheeling Goalie." Tosh.0. Comedy Central; 30 June 2010.
"Celia Sasic." FIFA.com. FIFA; 2015.
"Christen Press' Story- One Nation. One Team. 23 Stories." One
Nation One Team. US Soccer; 2015.
"Christie Rampone's Story- One Nation. One Team. 23 Stories."
One Nation One Team. US Soccer; 2015.

"Darling Issue No. 12 features #USWNT." US Soccer; 4 June 2015.

"Do You Know the Factors Influencing Girls' Participation in Sports?" Women's Sports Foundation; 7 June 2012.

Fagan, Kate. "In Other News… Oh Yeah, the Women's World Cup Starts Soon." ESPNW. ESPN; 27 May 2015.

"Farewell, Captain America: Five Things About Christie Rampone." US Soccer; 13 February 2017.

Ford, Bonnie D. "Marta's Quest for Soccer Glory." ESPNW. ESPN; 10 June 2015.

"Former US national team member Whitney Engen steps away from NWSL." ESPNW. Associated Press; 6 February 2017.

"Former US star Heather O'Reilly signs with Arsenal." Sports Illustrated; 18 January 2017.

"Former USWNT star Lauren Holiday in recovery after surgery for brain tumor." Sports Illustrated; 25 October 2016.

"#GirlUp" Youtube.com. Niagara Water; 19 June 2015.

Glock, Allison. "Pride. Regret. Hope." ESPNW. ESPN; 1 June 2015.

Gordon, James Bridget. "Ali Krieger's Move to Orlando Exposes Underlying Tension in Women's Soccer." Paste Magazine; 3 November 2016.

Hamm, Mia. "Quote by Mia Hamm." GoodReads.com; 2015.

Hays, Graham. "Different roads lead Morgan Brian, Lindsey Horan to starring roles in US midfield." ESPNW; 2 March 2016.

Hays, Graham. "Shannon Boxx, Lori Chalupny Retire From USWNT On Their Terms." ESPNW; 25 October 2015.

"Heath to ESPN: 'I Am Very Happy Here In The US.'" The Equilizer; 14 December 2016.

"Heather O'Reilly's Story- One Nation. One Team. 23 Stories." One Nation One Team. US Soccer; 2015.

Henley, William Earnest. "Invictus." Football's Christen Press; 3 April 2013.

"Hope Solo." Biography.com. A&E Entertainment; 2015.

"Julie Johnston's Story- One Nation. One Team. 23 Stories." One Nation One Team. US Soccer; 2015.

"Kelley O'Hara Named to 2016 US Women's Soccer Team." Sky Blue FC. National Women's Soccer League; 12 July 2016.

"Kelley O'Hara's Story- One Nation. One Team. 23 Stories." One Nation One Team. US Soccer; 2015.

"Klingenberg, Press, Sauerbrunn Elected USWNTPA Reps." The Equilizer; 3 February 2017.

Lacey, Ryan. "Louisa Necib: 5 Fast Facts You Need to Know." Heavy.com; 24 June 2015.

"Lauren Holiday Voted 2014 U.S. Female Soccer Athlete of the Year." US Soccer; 2014.

"Lori Chalupney's Story- One Nation. One Team. 23 Stories." One Nation One Team. US Soccer; 2015.

"Megan Rapinoe's Story- One Nation. One Team. 23 Stories." One Nation One Team. US Soccer; 2015.

"Meghan Klingenberg's- One Nation. One Team. 23 Stories." One Nation One Team. US Soccer; 2015.

"Morgan Brian's Story- One Nation. One Team. 23 Stories." One Nation One Team. US Soccer; 2015.

Mundo Sisters. "What Makes Us: 'Pinoe." ESPNW. ESPN; 2015.

Mundo Sisters. "What Makes Us: 'Vero'." ESPNW. ESPN; 2015.

Murray, Caitlin. "Why Hope Solo and Megan Rapinoe were left out of the USWNT roster for the SheBelieves Cup." Fox Sports; 8 February 2017.

Oxenham, Gwendolyn. "Anthropology of Soccer." 13 June 2015. Joseph C Wilson. Email Correspondence.

Oxenham, Gwendolyn. "Brazil's Neymar and Marta: Two 'Magicians,' Two Very Different Stories." Littlefield, Bill. NPR; 13 June 2015.

Peters, Justin. "World Cup Jerkwatch: Hope Solo is an Abrasive, Ayn-Rand Loving Reality Star Wannabe." Slate.com. Slate Magazine; 8 June 2015.

"Pregame Coverage." Fox Sports; 15 June 2015.

Rampone, Christie. "This is 40." The Players' Tribune; 12 June 2015.

Robinson, Matthew. "Tickets for final in high demand." Vancouver Sun.; 4 July 2015.

Rogers, Martin. "Alex Morgan, coach respond to Colombia star's bold comments." USA Today; 20 June 2015.

"Roster." US Soccer; 8 March 2017.

Schaerlaeckens, Leander. "'Babe City': How Sexist Coverage of the US Women's Soccer Team is Dying." Vice Sports; 30 June 2015.

Schaerlaeckens, Leander. "Don't Worry, Score Happy: How Christen Press Became a Budding U.S. Soccer Star." Vice Sports; 12 June 2015.

Schaerlaeckens, Leander. "The Girls who Escaped from the Taliban and Became a Soccer Star." Vice Sports; 10 June 2015.

Scurry, Briana. "Voices: Soccer Scandal is Black Butt Over Women's World Cup." USA Today; 28 May 2015.

Serwetnyk, Carrie. "Americans will bring extra emotion to rev up showdown." Vancouver Sun; 4 July 2015.

"Shannon Boxx's Story- One Nation. One Team. 23 Stories." One Nation One Team. US Soccer; 2015.

Shakespeare, William. "Prologue. Henry V." Shakespeare. MIT; 17 July 2015.

Shenfeld, Hilary. "See Soccer Star Julie Johnston Shop for Wedding Dresses as She Talks Prepping for the Rio Olympics: 'It's a Really Busy Summer!'" People Magazine; 21 June 2016.

"Sydney Leroux's Story- One Nation. One Team. 23 Stories." One Nation One Team. US Soccer; 2015.

"The backups find themselves vying for the starting spot going into the SheBelieves Cup finale against France on Tuesday." The Goal; 7 March 2017.

"A Title IX Primer." Women's Sports Foundation; 2011.

"Tobin Heath's Story- One Nation. One Team. 23 Stories." One Nation One Team. US Soccer; 2015.

"Whitney Engen's Story- One Nation. One Team. 23 Stories." One Nation One Team. US Soccer; 2015.

Yang, Stephanie. "Amy Rodriguez pregnant with second child, out for 2016 Olympics." Stars and Stripes FC. VOX Media; 2 January 2016.